REMEMBER WHEN

REMEMBER WHEN

A Nostalgic Look at America's National Pastime

Thomas S. Owens

Featuring Photographs from Corbis-Bettmann

MetroBooks

An Imprint of Friedman/Fairfax Publishers

© 1996 by Michael Friedman Publishing Group, Inc.

Library of Congress Cataloging-in-Publication data available upon request.

ISBN 1-56799-392-3

Editor: Stephen Slaybaugh
Art Director: Lynne Yeamans
Designer: Joseph Rutt
Photography Editor: Samantha Larrance
Photography Researcher: Darrell Perry

Color separations by Ocean Graphic International Company Ltd.
Printed in China by Leefung-Asco Printers Ltd.

For bulk purchases and special sales, please contact:
Friedman/Fairfax Publishers
Attention: Sales Department
15 West 26th Street
New York, NY 10010
212/685-6610 FAX 212/685-1307

Visit the Friedman/Fairfax Website:
http://www.webcom.com/friedman

DEDICATION

This book is dedicated to Diana Star Helmer,
All-Star Wife and MVP (Most Valuable Partner).

ACKNOWLEDGMENTS

This book was made possible through the efforts of editor Steve Slaybaugh and
first reader Diana Star Helmer. Kevin Whitver and Ray Medeiros lent their enthusiasm and
expertise, proving that baseball's future is in its past.

CONTENTS

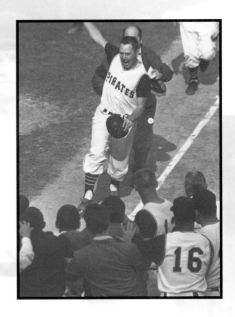

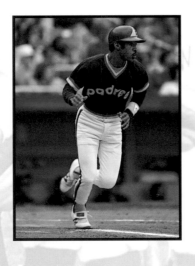

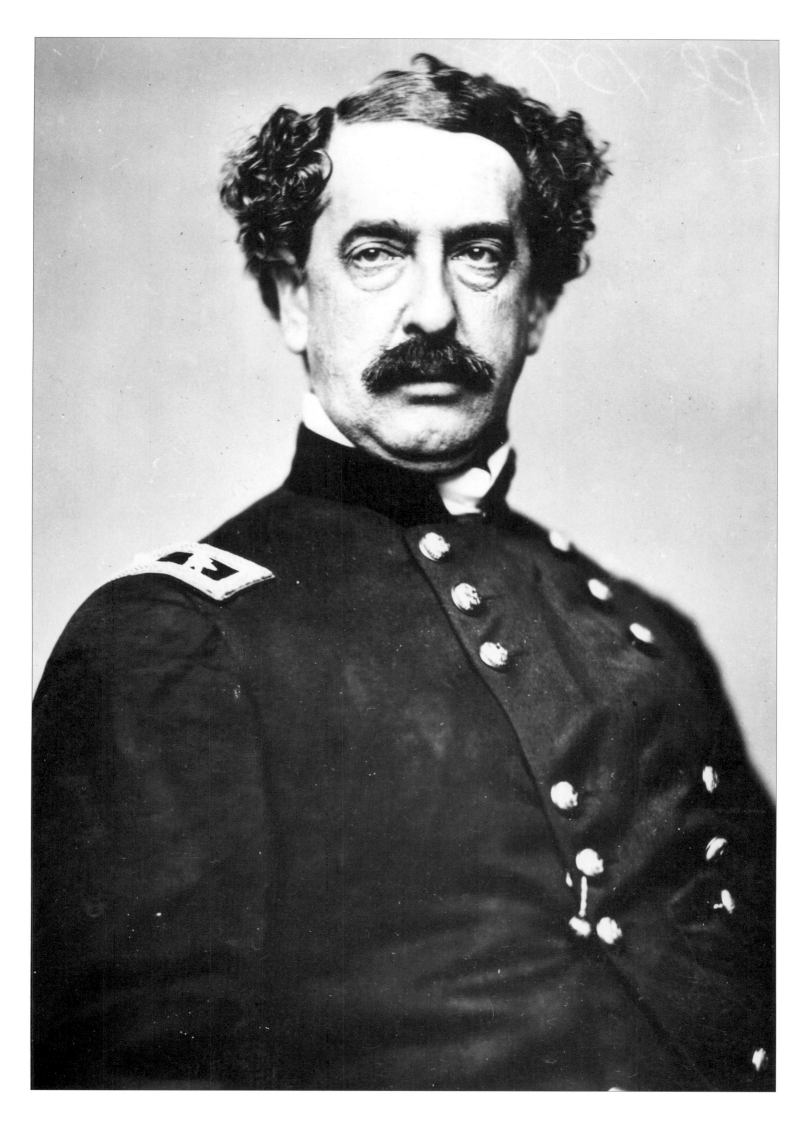

CHAPTER ONE

BASEBALL'S BEGINNINGS

"**M**y affection for the game still exists, however, and I am confident that purged of the many evils that now exist, the game itself will continue to be in the future what it has been in the past, the National Game of the American People."

How many recently retired stars might offer the same appraisal of Major League Baseball? The belief that pro ball is flawed, but pure at its core, is timeless. Fans might easily imagine an ex-player uttering these words following the strike-plagued 1990s, the drug scandals of the 1980s, or the free-agent battles of the 1970s, yet Adrian "Cap" Anson proffered this opinion in 1900 in his autobiography, *A Ball Player's Career; Being the Personal Experiences and Reminiscences of Adrian C. Anson, Late Manager and Captain of the Chicago Base Ball Club.*

Anson has been credited as the sport's first universally acknowledged superstar. He was the first player to record his perspectives of the game in print, views that are all the more valuable today because of the scarcity of published material during the time when professional baseball was just beginning. Even so, heroes' histories are often fueled by mythology and misinformation, and Anson's story of baseball's beginnings is no exception.

That the British games of cricket and rounders inspired early incarnations of baseball was taken for granted by many people. However, jingoistic pride fueled the generation of an all-American mythology about baseball's birth.

Baseball's revisionist history has insisted that Abner Doubleday devised the game in 1839 in Cooperstown, New York, instructing other youths in his custom-made sport. Supposedly, he adapted the game of Town Ball (which utilized twenty to fifty players) by offering modifications of bases, a standardized playing field, and a limit of eleven players per side.

OPPOSITE: *Just ten years after his death, Abner Doubleday was (incorrectly) dubbed the "Father of Baseball." This photograph of the Civil War hero was taken by Matthew Brady. While Major General Doubleday's military service was documented in various diaries, he never took credit for creating the sport.*

OVERLEAF: *This 1866 Currier and Ives lithograph offers a pastoral vision of early baseball at New Jersey's Elysian Fields. Observe the batter's divided grip, the pitcher's submarine delivery, and the outfield crowd's interpretation of "standing room only."*

Could Doubleday have been teaching a newly devised recreation to school chums in 1839? Hardly. Starting his second year as a cadet at the U.S. Military Academy, Doubleday was required to remain at West Point that year or face AWOL charges. Doubleday's military heroism in both the Mexican and Civil Wars probably gave him his place in baseball lore: early doubters of his contributions found their protests quelled by patriotism.

But a New York bank teller named Alexander Joy Cartwright was the legitimate father of modern baseball. Beginning in 1842, Cartwright participated in regular baseball games with other white-collar types at New York's Madison Square. In September 1845, he organized his fellow volunteer firefighters along with other athletic companions to form the New York Knickerbockers, the first publicly declared baseball team. The Knickerbockers adopted bylaws and a constitution.

The Knickerbockers' 1848 charter was more than game regulations. They formalized a code of honor, agreeing to abide by a list of penalties that required fines of 6¼ to 50 cents for using profane language, debating with umpires, or disobeying the team captain.

Subsequently, Cartwright helped develop a rule book, setting game times at 9 innings (instead of "aces," playing until a team scored 21 runs), and lengthening base paths to ninety feet. Three outs per side, a preset batting order, and nine players per lineup were other Cartwright-led innovations. Most important, baseball developed an initial—though temporary—reputation as a gentlemanly game, thanks to Cartwright's rule of forbidding throwing at base runners and batters to put them out. Previously, "soakball" had been a popular baseball variation, in which dodging balls thrown by fielders was the only accepted method for being called safe, both literally and competitively.

Cartwright's crew had immediate practical reasons for distinguishing fair from foul territory. Because of urban development, space for playing

Henry Chadwick, seventy-eight years old in this 1902 portrait, could be considered the sport's first beat reporter. His later inventions of scorekeeping and the box score guaranteed fan attendance for contests like this championship match between the Philadelphia Athletics and Brooklyn Atlantics in 1866.

fields was limited. The Knickerbockers adopted Hoboken, New Jersey, as their home turf, playing at Elysian Fields weekly.

In 1849, Cartwright headed west for California's gold rush, teaching the game en route to anyone willing to learn. All sorts of people, from Native Americans to soldiers and farmers, became baseball players under Cartwright's tutelage. After his stay in California, Cartwright set sail for China, but because of dysentery, he settled in Honolulu. Before his death in 1892, Cartwright had introduced baseball to the Hawaiian Islands long before many mainlanders had experienced the game.

But Cartwright's acts did not speak as strongly to nineteenth-century Americans as did the words of Manifest Destiny. Fears of foreign influence on baseball's origin resulted in support for the Doubleday creation theory long before it was refined in the subsequent century.

Consider the 1888 book *Base-ball, How to Become a Player, With the Origin, History and Explanation of the Game* by John Montgomery Ward of the New York Base-ball Club. Ward stated that by 1856 "the fact became apparent that [baseball] was surely superseding the English game of cricket, and the adherents of the latter game looked with ill-concealed jealousy on the rising upstart. There were

then, as now, persons who believed that everything good and beautiful in this world must be of English origin, and these at once felt the need of a pedigree for the new game." Ward used comments from two original members of Cartwright's Knickerbockers to further claims that the American-spawned baseball was thriving before 1800.

Although Cartwright's contributions to the growth of organized baseball are well documented, no one person can claim to have invented the sport. Pilgrims played versions of cricket in the early 1600s. Through the 1800s, baseball evolved with participation from players of all ages and social classes.

In 1857, "The New York Game" was a common label for the sport. Delegates from sixteen teams from the area convened to adopt one set of rules to govern the games of all clubs represented. In 1859, Amherst hosted what would be considered the first intercollegiate baseball game, thumping Williams, 73–32.

Even the Civil War had but a dampening effect on the game's growth. In 1866, Ward stated that delegates from 202 clubs in seventeen states attended the loosely formed National Association's annual convention. Paying fans flocked to see games, while teams continued to claim that their

This 1899 woodcut depicts a play at second base in a New York–Brooklyn contest at the Polo Grounds. Even before photography was common and affordable, newspapers knew that fans craved new perspectives on the game.

stars were unpaid amateurs who shared only in a percentage of gate receipts.

In 1866, surging attendance was evidenced at the association's championship match between the Brooklyn Atlantics and the Philadelphia Athletics. For the first time, printed scorecards were sold. Although only eight thousand tickets were sold at 25 cents apiece, one newspaper estimated that attendance exceeded thirty thousand spectators. The Philadelphia opener was canceled when the overflowing crowd clogged the field. Replayed in Brooklyn before nineteen thousand fans, the Atlantics won, 27–17.

The association abandoned the practice of players playing without pay in 1868. "By making this distinction it would no longer be considered a disgrace for an amateur to be beaten by a professional nine," Ward wrote. "For the professionals, the change was most beneficial. It legitimized their occupation and left them at liberty to pursue openly and honorably what they had been forced to follow under false colors."

Besides the new cost of player salaries, teams had to contend with the fact that players wouldn't be viewed forever as fun-loving innocents who played the game for mere recreation. What had once been a game was suddenly a business.

Pitching became the first area where sophistication emerged. Initially, batters were allowed to request where they desired their pitches to arrive. Early incarnations of the game referred to the "server," who had an unofficial obligation to assist the batter in getting a pitch that could be hit. Not until a strike zone was defined in 1887 was that practice discarded.

Jim Creighton, considered baseball's first professional by some historians, was one of its first mavericks because of his legendary fastballs. Although rules essentially limited pitchers to underhand and submarine (slow overhand) deliveries, Creighton's offerings were marked by rising speed. He gained recognition in 1858–1859 while pitching for the Brooklyn Niagras and Excelsiors. The right-hander was an all-around success, but he died from internal bleeding a few days after belting a home run. Historians now believe that the fallen hero may have suffered a ruptured spleen while overswinging. He was twenty-one.

William Arthur Cummings, known as "Candy," was baseball's first famous curveballer. In 1863, the fourteen-year-old observed the trajectory of clam shells he tossed. To counter the criticism that he was deceiving batters, the righty said that because of his five-foot-nine-inch, 120-pound frame, he

These Cincinnati refugees kept their "Red Stockings" moniker initially, along with their reputation as baseball's first professional dynasty.

needed the specialty pitch to compete against larger, stronger opponents. Although legendary sportswriter Henry Chadwick admitted that he had witnessed the trick pitch a decade earlier, he still proclaimed Cummings the first to master the breaking ball.

Ironically, all pitchers of the era, not just Cummings and Creighton, escape criticism of their lack of control. Because rules required 9 balls for a walk, hitters knew that their options were limited.

Meanwhile, player options broadened in 1869 with the creation of the Cincinnati Red Stockings, the first acknowledged professional team in the sport's history.

The public knew that the players came from different parts of the country—not just Cincinnati—and that the entire roster drew salaries. The highest-paid player was George Wright, the brother of manager Harry. The team was unbeatable, ending the season with a perfect 65–0 mark. The team claimed another famous first as well: the Cincinnati groundskeeper was the first to realize that a field could be marked out with chalk lines, ending the practice of digging furrows that made everlasting foul lines.

The 1870 Red Stockings risked a 92-game winning streak against the hosting Brooklyn Atlantics on June 14. At the end of 9 innings, the Brooklynites stated satisfaction with the 5–5 tie and assumed a draw. However, Cincinnati manager Harry Wright flashed his mastery of the rules, insisting on extra innings. Two innings later, 2 fielding errors produced an 8–7 win for Brooklyn and an eventual financial collapse for "the Cincinnatis," as Wright dubbed the team when telegramming the sad news back to Ohio.

The *Cincinnati Gazette* issued a premature obituary for the burgeoning sport, stating: "The baseball mania has run its course. It has no future as a professional endeavor."

Quite the opposite proved true. The willingness of the public to pay to watch baseball resulted in newspapers sarcastically appraising "shooting stars" and "revolvers," star players who would abandon teams for better-paying clubs. Free agency, it seems, was a part of baseball from the start.

The gap between the amateur and pro teams widened in 1871. The National Association finally divided ranks, with the professional sector comprising nine teams. Well-known baseball havens like

The Philadelphia Athletics remained one of baseball's most stable and enduring franchises. This woodcut captures the 1874 squad.

On and off the field, Adrian Constantine Anson was recognized in many circles as baseball's first superstar. "Cap" is remembered for introducing the ritual of spring training. His opposition to black players in pro ball wasn't examined fully until after he became a charter member of the Baseball Hall of Fame.

Boston, Philadelphia, New York, and Chicago were joined by locales such as Troy, New York; Fort Wayne, Indiana; and Rockford, Illinois.

In the first five years of its existence, the National Association of Professional Base Ball Players gave four league crowns to the Boston Red Stockings. The same team that had abandoned Cincinnati because of fading fan and investor support had been invited by Boston backers to move east; Captain Wright and his cronies even took the team name with them.

While America celebrated its centennial in 1876, another milestone was passed in baseball, all because William Ambrose Hulbert, majority owner of the Chicago White Stockings, hoped for an instant winner.

Hulbert engaged in the dubious practice of offering secret contracts to already-signed players from opposing clubs. Boston's star pitcher, Albert Goodwill Spalding, was the first to jump ship, eventually convincing three Red Stockings teammates and Philadelphia's Cap Anson to join Hulbert, too. The players, as well as the entire team, risked being expelled from the National Association for team-jumping, so Hulbert built a new league around his club in the autumn of 1875: the

National League of Professional Base Ball Clubs. Cincinnati, Louisville, and St. Louis were the first additions, with Hartford, Philadelphia, Boston, and New York joining in February 1876. Their first season of play was the year that America turned one hundred.

The White Stockings' 52–14 record topped the league, contrasted by the last-place mark of Cincinnati at 9–56.

The National League began retaining individual statistics in 1879. However, stolen bases, as well as a pitcher's walks, strikeouts, and hit batsmen, weren't recorded officially until 1886. The run batted in wouldn't become universal until the twentieth century, leading sportswriters to review old box scores to figure past RBI.

Baseball had a rowdy reputation in the 1880s; it wasn't an amusement that most gentlemen took their wives and daughters to. Yet the decade wasn't without its inspiring role models, including Billy Sunday, whose many on-field accomplishments were actually overshadowed by his fervent Christian proclamations.

In 1881, Sunday was a player in Marshalltown, Iowa, for the team's semipro club, the Ansons. Cap Anson credited his Aunt Em with

ABOVE: *When fans proved their willingness to support a team financially, the clubs responded with then-modern facilities like the "new" grounds of the metropolitan baseball club in Staten Island, New York.*

OPPOSITE: *As baseball's popularity boomed, once-practical equipment became male fashion statements. Long before uniform numbers were needed to tell team members apart, caps helped fans distinguish the players of one team from another.*

discovering the speedy high school student. Whether teaching Bible school or crediting God's influence for his baseball talents, Sunday was always making news. He premiered with the 1883 White Stockings, his first of three teams. In his final season, with Pittsburgh and Philadelphia in 1890, Sunday racked up 84 stolen bases.

Still in his twenties, Sunday strayed from baseball, choosing a full-time job in religion. A hellfire-and-brimstone evangelist, Sunday attracted thousands to his revivals and tent meetings. Preaching in Marshalltown (population 13,300), the town founded by Cap Anson's father, Sunday attracted crowds exceeding 200,000. A welcoming parade was viewed by ten thousand spectators. One of Sunday's first goals as a gospel standard-bearer was to eliminate all Sunday baseball games.

During one Iowa appearance, Sunday told a crowd about a nameless ex-player in Chicago who had tried to convert to Christianity before his death. Sunday illustrated his point by diving headfirst toward the base of the pulpit. "You see, a deathbed conversion is a lot like trying to stretch a triple into a home run. I might have done that sometimes when I played ball, but I only had the home plate umpire to worry about." His conversion pitch ended with, "But this time, the Real Umpire is there. And he says, 'You're Out!'"

Sunday never turned his back on baseball entirely, however. As he toured the country to hold evening revivals, the minister had free time during many of his days. In the towns he visited, Sunday was a frequent umpire for semipro contests.

The greatest against-all-odds tale of the 1800s may belong to William Ellsworth Hoy. Because he had meningitis as an infant, the Ohio-born Hoy became a deaf-mute, and he was known as "Dummy" during his playing career. Yet Hoy completed his grammar school and high school education at the Ohio School for the Deaf in a mere six years, and graduated as class valedictorian.

His pro career began in 1886 with a Northwest League team from Oshkosh, Wisconsin. Home plate umpires accommodated the five-foot-four-inch, 148-pound center fielder with hand signals for balls and strikes,

BASE BALL CAPS.

No. 5. Chicago Style.
4 Qualities.

No. 19. Skull Cap.
5 Qualities.

Cheap Muslin Cap.
Lined.   Unlined.

BASE BALL CAPS.

No. 4. Eton.
3 Qualities.

No. 11. Jockey Style.
5 Qualities.

No. 13. Boston Style with Star.
5 Qualities.

BASE BALL CAPS

No. 7. Boston Style.
5 Qualities.

No. 21. College Cap.
Cheap Felt, Lined.   Cheap Felt, Unlined.

No. 21. College Style.
5 Qualities.

BASE BALL CAPS.

No. T. L. Tennis Style.
4-inch Visor.

No. E. L. Eaton Style.
4-inch Visor.

No. N. Norwood Style.

beginning an unofficial tradition. A fleet-footed fielder famed for playing shallow, Hoy became the first flyhawker ever to throw out three runners trying to score in 1 game (June 19, 1888). His fourteen-year career, beginning with the '88 Washington Senators, included stays in the National League, Players League, American Association, and American League.

Another diamond nobleman was John Montgomery Ward, the author of the aforementioned 1888 book. He broke into the sport with Providence in 1878, logging a league-finest 44 wins as an eighteen-year-old. Two years later, he pitched baseball's second perfect game. Earning a law degree from Penn State during his career, Ward's sense of justice led him to form baseball's first union, the Players' Brotherhood. As all players were being contractually tied to one team for life by the reserve clause, Ward then organized a rival Players League. But the league lasted only through 1890 and did little to loosen the owner's financial stranglehold.

Owners took the opportunity to cap player salaries (limiting top pay to $2,500) when labor leader Ward was out of the country. He was part of the all-star barnstorming team created by new White Stockings owner Al Spalding in 1889. In hopes of making baseball an international affair, the group mounted exhibitions in Australia, Egypt, Italy, and Great Britain.

To welcome the party back to the United States, a New York banquet was held and was attended by Teddy Roosevelt and Mark Twain. The night was filled with proclamations that the trip proved that there was nothing like baseball anywhere in the world. "No rounders!" was the cry from the banquet's attendees.

Mark Twain spoke eloquently at the banquet of baseball's achievements, and another writer took the sport to even greater heights in the entertainment world in 1888: the *San Francisco Examiner* was the first to publish Ernest Thayer's epic, "Casey at the Bat: A Ballad of the Republic."

Throughout America, more innovations began to blossom. The fielding glove and the catcher's mask were auditioned by several players in 1875. Pete Browning, the 1882 batting champion of the American Association and star of the Louisville Eclipse, revolutionized batting in 1884. He found a local woodworker named Bud Hillerich to customize a bat, soon to be baptized the Louisville Slugger. Of course, sportswriter Chadwick had invented the box score and created the scoring system that is still in use today. The 1888 Red Stockings wore numbers on their sleeves. (Experiments to distinguish position players by different colors of uniforms had failed.)

The changing times brought about changing faces, too. Louisville Colonels third baseman Jeremiah Denny retired after the 1894 season. Not only was Denny adept at throwing with either hand, but the gloveless veteran was the league's last remaining barehand-fielding player.

Following Anson's forced 1897 retirement (when the team reneged on a deal to allow him to buy a controlling interest in the club), Chadwick penned a tribute in the 1898 league guide. Looking beyond statistics, Chadwick waxed, "Almost alone, as a minority man, he stood by the National League in its greatest hour of need, in opposition to the desertion of hundreds of his confrères in the League ranks. In these prominent characters, we say, Anson stands… unique in the annals of the professional fraternity." No mention was made of Anson's landmark feat, becoming the first player to reach 3,000 lifetime hits.

Little did Chadwick know that Anson's greatest off-field accomplishment would wind up being the innovation of spring training, when he assembled his 1887 club for a training camp in Hot Springs, Arkansas. As a manager, he was a visionary, employing such unheard-of techniques as resting pitchers on a rotation basis.

Anson's father, Henry Anson, gave an interview to the Marshalltown, Iowa, *Times-Republican* newspaper. "I would prefer to see him retire from base ball altogether, leave Chicago and come back to Marshalltown to live," the elder Anson stated, adding that he hoped his son would "join me in the upbuilding of the city." With fatherly pride, he concluded, "As far as his ball playing is concerned, I think he is as capable of playing good ball as he ever did in his life. If not better. He has as much, if not more, muscle and brain than he ever possessed, and every one knows that it takes both to play nowadays. But he has won honor and glory enough and is entitled to retire."

Anson's retirement also helped rename the Chicago club. Without "old Anse" at the helm, the Colts (post–White Stockings, from 1890 to 1897) were known as the Chicago Orphans

Before his 1935 death, Billy Sunday gained glory as a fiery evangelist and flamboyant preacher. Although Sunday ended his playing career with the 1890 Pirates, he was known to occasionally umpire afternoon semipro games before his evening tent revivals.

from 1898 to 1901. Curiously, the Colts name drew from Anson's appearance in the stage play *Runaway Colt.*

Team names seemed to change almost as frequently as rosters. The pre-1885 Giants were christened the Gothams. The Brooklyn Grays (1884–1888) transformed into the Bridegrooms (1889–1898) and then into the Superbas (1899–1904). The Boston Red Caps (1876–1882) were refitted as the Beaneaters (1883–1906). Prior to 1891, the Pirates were known first as the Alleghenies, then as the Innocents. After coaxing player Lou Bierbauer to leave Philadelphia, the Pirates moniker was no longer considered a compliment.

Both baseball's names and rules were changing. The pitcher's box moved from forty-five to fifty feet in 1881. Overhand pitching was mandated in 1884, with the 3-strikes-you're-out idea passing in 1888. The 4-ball walk was accepted in 1889. In 1893, the distance for the recently added mound increased to today's sixty feet six inches when a surveyor goofed reading the blueprint. A year later, foul balls began counting for a batter's first 2 strikes. The infield fly rule followed in 1895.

However, the twentieth century was waiting with baseball's biggest change of all: the addition of the American League.

CHAPTER TWO

1900–1909

T he National League would not remain *the* major league for long. Four losing, poorly attended clubs—the Washington Senators, Baltimore Orioles, Cleveland Spiders, and Louisville Colonels—were cut loose from the parent organization in 1899. In their 1899 finales, other rival owners sensed the death knell for the four franchises and lured the most talented players to their more prosperous clubs. Back to eight teams, the NL faced a paltry existence in 1900. The schedule was slashed to 140 games.

The National League's first season of the twentieth century was decided with a playoff between the Brooklyn Superbas (named after a circus act) and the Pittsburgh Pirates, the first- and second-place teams, respectively. The Pirates were outgunned, although they finished only 3 wins shy of the Brooklynites' 82–54 regular-season output.

Through it all, owners fought over how to split ticket money between the two teams, engaging in several lawsuits along the way.

Byron Bancroft Johnson, president of the most successful minor league in the country, saw his chance to move into the majors in 1900. He adopted cities abandoned by the National League, placing teams of his own there. Even while signing out-of-work talent from exiled NL clubs, Johnson criticized the established loop's restrictive draft rules that inhibited other clubs from acquiring players. The Protective Association of Professional Baseball Players was another new organization, unionlike in its intent to protect the value of the dwindling berths on remaining teams.

Charles Comiskey, owner of a minor league team in St. Paul, was allowed into the Johnson's new American League with Chicago's second team. Suddenly, the 1901 cities of Boston, Chicago, and St. Louis each hosted two professional teams. When players began jumping ship to join the upstart AL, National League attendance sank.

OPPOSITE: *New York pitcher Christy Mathewson poses for a portrait in 1905.*

The inaugural AL season wasn't short on excitement. Active since 1890 and known as "Cy," Denton True Young was the league's leading pitcher with 33 victories; he would pace the junior circuit in wins for two more years. His nickname stemmed from "Cyrus" (slang for a naive country boy), but writers later assumed the title was short for Cyclone. Before retiring in 1911, he was called "Foxy Grandpa" by other players in the league.

Lajoie was king of the American League. He won the Triple Crown with numbers of .422, 14 home runs, and 125 RBI. (His batting average was aided somewhat by the AL's slowness to adopt the rule that "any foul ball not caught on a fly is a strike unless the batter has 2 strikes on him," which the National League incorporated in 1901. AL hitters didn't face this adaptation until 1903.)

Both leagues saw the shape of the game change in 1900, when home plate switched from a twelve-inch square to a five-sided base seventeen inches wide.

Just who were the first American Leaguers? Their team names included:

The Puritans. Sometimes called the Pilgrims, this was Boston's first AL squad. To honor temporary head boss Charles Somers, the team tinkered with the name "Somersets." However, a change of ownership in 1907 would convert the club into the Red Stockings.

The Milwaukee Brewers. After a first season in Wisconsin, the team moved to St. Louis, adopting the leftover Browns name from the defunct American Association entity.

In Cleveland, fans may have needed scorecards to track the team name. The Broncos name evolved into the Blues, after the adoption of new club colors. Calling the team "the Naps" made sense, as long as player-manager Napoleon Lajoie was in charge (which was the case until 1915, when Nap left the team and the Indians moniker was chosen).

The American League's good fortune dogged the National League in 1902. NL players continued to stray to AL teams. But when the two Philadelphia teams, the Phillies and the Athletics, battled in the Pennsylvania Supreme Court over legal rights to players, a small off-field victory went to the older league. The state ruled that Lajoie was bound to his prior three-year contract with Philadelphia. In a more tangible show of NL strength, Cincinnati enjoyed the

decade in a lush new ballpark called "Palace of the Fans."

Of course, the National League had Christy Mathewson to depend on. "Matty" premiered in 1900, one year out of Bucknell University. After going 0–3, his purchase by the New York Giants was canceled. The Reds promptly drafted Mathewson for $100, then swapped him to New York for faded moundsman Amos Rusie.

Through 1909, Mathewson averaged 27 triumphs yearly. In addition, his good looks, model work ethic, and spotless lifestyle made him perfect as a role model to kids. His career was summed up by Bozeman Bulger, a New York *Evening World* writer: "In addition to physical ability, Mathewson had the perfect temperament for a ballplayer. Always, he sought to learn something new, and he never forgot what he had learned in the past. He had everything— strength, intelligence, courage and willingness."

Back in the American League, the second official season proved that "the junior circuit's" level of play could compete with any other league. Athletics outfielder Ralph "Socks" Seybold walloped a loop-best 16 home runs. Meanwhile, Pittsburgh's Tommy Leach was the NL leader with 6 round-trippers. Incidentally, Seybold's total matched Cincinnati outfielder Sam Crawford's 1901 tally. The joint mark would remain a high through 1909. Crawford was renamed "Wahoo Sam" after his hometown of Wahoo, Nebraska.

While Philadelphia won the AL crown by a mere 5 games, the Pirates' 103 victories gave them the senior circuit title by a 27½- game margin. By contrast, only 9 victories separated first through fourth place in the American League. The AL's financial dominance and popularity with fans at the end of the "aught-two" season forced the National League to realize that it wasn't as dominant a force in baseball as it once was. Pirates owner Harry Pulliam was appointed NL president, and a peace treaty between

ABOVE: *The annual* Reach Baseball Guide *contained more than statistics. The photos captured the hearts and minds of fans before the age of television. This panorama details the second game of the 1905 World Series at New York City's Polo Grounds, with the Athletics afield.*

LEFT: *Christy Mathewson was a Polo Grounds mainstay. His dominance for the decade was capped by a 1.14 ERA in 1909. Celebrated by the press, this moundsman baffled right-handed hitters with his cunning and his fadeaway change-up.*

the two leagues, the National Agreement, was signed in January 1903.

The term seemed appropriate, as the senior circuit knew that it faced defeat in a losing battle for finances. A three-member national commission panel of AL head Johnson, NL chief Harvey Pulliam, and commission chair Garry Herrmann (the Cincinnati owner, who held a tie-breaking vote) oversaw the coexistence of the leagues. But Pulliam would not live to see baseball in the teens; he suffered a nervous breakdown and, on June 28, 1909, shot himself in the head at age forty.

Yet Pulliam's influence on baseball was substantial. The marriage of powers was highlighted by the first-ever World Series, in which the Boston Red Sox bested the Pirates in 5 out of 9 games, overcoming a 3-games-to-1 deficit.

One interesting note during the 1903 season was the old Baltimore Orioles franchise pulling up stakes. The team transferred to New York to become

the Highlanders. Within a decade, the team name would become the New York Yankees. The team's transfer was the last that any team would make for the next fifty years: all major league cities would keep the same clubs in the same locations until 1953.

As gloves became more sophisticated and pitching kept improving, the "deadball" era developed into lower-scoring games filled with all types of defensive innovations. Jay "Nig" Clarke, Cleveland's rookie catcher, quietly sported soccer guards beneath his socks in 1905. The same year, New York's Roger Bresnahan tried batting while wearing a pneumatic head protector to recover from a beaning. But it was Bresnahan's great catching in 1907, using now-familiar shin guards, that made the future Hall of Famer famous.

Baseball managers were gaining their own reputations. Philadelphia manager Cornelius McGillicuddy, known to the sporting world as "Connie Mack," was

RIGHT: *Mathewson's battery mate was Roger Bresnahan, a slick-fielding catcher known for introducing shin guards in 1907. The catcher's Irish roots earned him the nickname "The Duke of Tralee."*

dubbed "The Tall Tactician." Cubs player-manager Frank Chance, once known as "Husk," turned into "the Peerless Leader." Detroit's general, Hughie Jennings, was christened "Ee-Yah" for the yells he hurled at opponents. Giants leader John McGraw became "Little Napoleon." The New York field leader did little to quell such dastardly depictions of his baseball philosophy. "With my team," he proclaimed, "I am an absolute czar."

McGraw had concluded his playing career in 1901, as player-manager of the Baltimore Orioles in the new league. He had been able to demand a contract without a reserve clause, freeing him from a lifetime obligation to one club. So after numerous battles with Byron Johnson over umpiring disputes and other protests raged on without conclusion, McGraw abandoned the Orioles. He was off to the senior-league Giants in mid-1902 to begin a three-decade association with the team.

It took less than three years for the scheming skipper to put a temporary hold on postseason play. In 1904, after McGraw's New York squad won a then-record 106 contests and the league pennant, he refused to allow his players to oppose Boston in "a defense of the world title" (McGraw's own boxing-term billing). Giants owner John Brush chimed in, saying that Boston was no more than a minor league champion. McGraw's refusal was a well-aimed attempt to humiliate the American League and its president. "Be in a hurry to win. Don't be in a hurry to lose," was one of McGraw's oft spoken credos.

What saved the World Series? The press pulverized McGraw and Brush, and players were peeved that they lost a chance to earn a share of the postseason gate. But in 1905, the Giants

squared off against the Athletics. Three shutouts by Mathewson preserved the club's reputation. And McGraw dressed his 1906 players in black uniforms with white letters that read "World's Champions."

An interrupted World Series wasn't the only heartbreak of 1904. Highlanders hurler Jack Chesbro became a pitching dynamo, compiling a 41–12 mark with 48 complete games and 454.2 innings pitched in 51 starts. However, when the ace lost his final outing to Boston on a wild pitch, New York's pennant hopes were crushed, losing by only 1½ games.

Without a doubt, the boom in pitching superiority underscored baseball's growing reputation as a thinking man's game. For a quarter century, the public would read about how conditions were constantly improving for players, with new equipment and refined rules. However, the plight of the umpire was overlooked until the twentieth century.

Umpire abuse was recognized by AL president Johnson as a growing problem in 1901. White Stockings shortstop Frank Shugart was banned for life for striking an ump. With only one umpire per game who would be distracted by watching the path of a batted ball, fielders and base runners saw unlimited invitations for all kinds of cheating.

Upon becoming an umpire for the National League in 1905, Bill Klem gave new color to the men in blue. Newspapers took notice not just of his umping, but of Klem's fiery personality. "It ain't nothin' til I call it," Klem proclaimed. First nicknamed "Catfish" for his facial features and later dubbed "The Old Arbitrator" for his lengthy service to the game, Klem developed a reputation for fearlessness. In the 1904 American Association, he used his spiked shoe to draw an actual line in the dirt. Even at five feet seven and a half inches and 157 pounds, Klem still managed to keep angry players and managers at bay. He pioneered the techniques of hand signals for fair or foul balls, and for home-plate umps standing at an angle behind the catcher to get better views of the strike zone.

Umpires weren't the only targets for abuse. In a throwback to the days of Roman chariots, visiting players would arrive at ballparks in uniform. After suiting up in hotel rooms, they would be taken to the game in horse-drawn carriages. After games, visiting players (now dirty and smelly) would depart in the same fashion. Finally, in 1906, Dodgers owner Charles Ebbets convinced the National League to provide dressing rooms for visiting teams. Although the ceremonial arrivals of opponents had often been picturesque, hometown fans too frequently enjoyed the opportunity to taunt foes, tossing everything imaginable at the passing player parade—which may be why, in 1909, all player parades were banned.

In 1908, the thrill of baseball was set to music. Lyricist Jack Norworth and composer Albert Von Tilzer wrote a song entitled "Take Me Out to the Ball Game." Fans swooned when the words to the song were included on illustrated slides in movie theaters.

Norworth and Von Tilzer weren't the only ones to combine song and the grand ol' game. Cap Anson and his two daughters toured briefly with their own stage act. The Anson ladies would pass out papier-mâché baseballs to the audience. In turn, the crowd would pitch to the aging superstar (who was wearing his old Chicago uniform) as he tried to swat their servings with a silver bat. Sportswriter Ring Lardner

OPPOSITE AND RIGHT: *John J. McGraw played for, and later managed, the New York Giants in his own gritty style. It was no accident that sportswriters nicknamed him "Little Napoleon." His aggressiveness stems from his contribution to the hit-and-run play.*

teamed with fabled Broadway performer George M. Cohan to create the act for the Anson family.

The words to the nearly forgotten verse are:

> Katie Casey was baseball mad, had the fever and had it bad.
> Just to root for the hometown crew, ev'ry sou—
> Katie blew.
> On a Saturday, her young beau
> called to see if she'd like to go,
> To see a show but Miss Kate said, "No,
> I'll tell you what you can do..."

Another change came over the public perception of baseball. For years, most newspaper writers had served as local cheerleaders. Then, during the 1908 World Series, visiting Detroit journalists in Chicago were offered some of the poorest seats in the park. To retaliate, Detroit placed Chicago scribes on the roof of the first-base stands to cover the game exposed to Chicago's torrid October weather.

The media's reaction was to form the Baseball Writers' Association of America. Not only did the organization encourage balanced treatment of reporters, but it tried to instill an objectivity in all writers. Even so, newspapers didn't rush to undo the accepted tradition of the club paying the traveling expenses of writers who covered the games.

The major leagues depended on writers to help convince the public that baseball was an all-American game. In 1907, two years of investigation by a panel of team officials and writers declared that baseball had been invented in Cooperstown by Abner Doubleday. The media, pandering to a patriotic public, ignored testimony from Henry Chadwick that the game was descended from British versions of cricket and rounders. Shortly afterward, the eighty-three-year-old Chadwick, known as the "Father of Baseball," contracted pneumonia after attending Brooklyn's chilly home opener, and died on April 20, 1908. He would be the last major figure for the next three decades to dispute baseball's concocted origins.

The 1909 Fall Classic offered hope for future adaptations in the game. After a prolonged rhubarb over whether a hit was fair or foul marred the third game between Detroit and Pittsburgh, the umping crew was doubled for the fourth game. While Klem retained his behind-the-plate roost (because of the respect paid him by players for strike calling) and Billy Evans oversaw the bases, Jimmy Johnstone and Silk O'Loughlin were employed to watch what passed the foul lines. O'Loughlin displayed the thick skin that umps of the decade needed to survive when he summed up his abilities: "The pope for religion, O'Loughlin for baseball. Both are infallible."

Umpires weren't the only controversial figures in baseball. Fans often experienced love-hate affairs with team owners. Oddly, fans for many years were dubbed "bugs," even "cranks" by the press. But *Brooklyn Eagle* newspaperman Tom Rice gave voice to fan complaints in print. He opined that scorecards should be free. After all, he reasoned, a program was free to each ticket holder at the theater. A team's scorecard was simply a roster surrounded by advertisements. Without public address systems in parks to announce changes, a scorecard seemed a necessity.

Another suggestion of Rice's was to have a board in each park that could list a lineup, the score per innings, and other happenings. Most ballparks utilized megaphone-wielding announcers who screamed out the lineups, hoping the press box could hear. George A. Baird invented the first electric scoreboard in 1908, but some teams held on to hand-operated versions for decades.

Fans began to get credit from the media for their spirited contributions to a team's success, and reporters mercifully shortened the term from "fanatics." Boston, winner of the first World Series, also boasted the first famed fans, the self-proclaimed "Royal Rooters" from Mike McGreevey's tavern. Operating from their base just outside the team's Huntington Grounds home,

Ring Lardner (left), seen with contemporary Gene Buck, acquired acclaim as a poetic baseball reporter. Besides covering games, Lardner's literary contributions to baseball included creating vaudeville skits.

McGreevey's patrons took fandom to new heights with banners, songs, and steady attendance.

Probably the greatest tribute to fans began with Shibe Park's opening in Philadelphia. The new structure was a cross between a castle and a cathedral, with an ornate steeple behind home plate. Within the domed tower were team mogul Connie Mack's offices. Surrounded on all four sides by strings of apartments, rooftop fans had the ultimate cheap seats. Even so, a roost within the stadium was often scarce during the Athletics' glory years, because of the scant twenty-thousand seat maximum.

Forbes Field followed in Pittsburgh, hosting its first contest on June 30, 1909. With a capacity of twenty-three thousand the triple-decked facility (with baseball's first elevator!) replaced Exposition Park, which had stood since 1900. Years later, the site became the grounds for Three Rivers stadium. Sensing a trend, Cleveland also updated its League Park, as did St. Louis its Sportsman's Park.

Baseball had entered the twentieth century dependent on rickety, outdated wooden parks. Stadium fires were commonplace; the public even suspected a baseball-hating firebug after three 1901 ballparks succumbed to flames within a two-month span. The condition of baseball's ballparks was brought into question after a tragedy in Philadelphia on August 6, 1903. Twelve fans died and 232 were injured as a section of rotten wooden railing for the bleachers collapsed.

Six years later, teams were flocking to improve their homes with structures displaying concrete and steel. Larger crowds made larger parks a necessity. As a result, even larger crowds flooded into these new showplaces.

RIGHT: *Umpire Bill Klem became baseball's first famed arbiter. Repeatedly claiming "I never missed one in my life," he later summed up his love for the job: "Baseball to me is not a game; it is a religion."*

There were sixteen major league teams to choose from, and attendance still rose. Despite the hope that all clubs could be box-office equals, no illusions existed over the widening on-field gap between winners and losers.

In the National League from 1901 to 1909, Pittsburgh owned four pennants, Chicago three, and New York two. The American Leaguers were composed of three Detroit pennants, and a pair of titles each from Boston, Philadelphia, and Chicago's White Stockings. Baseball's silent majority, nine different franchises, never tasted a first-place season throughout that first decade of rival leagues.

Although baseball's spoils wouldn't be spread among many more victors in the coming teens, an overhaul was due. The "deadball" era was about to come to a new end.

CHAPTER THREE

1910–1919

Although the National League was beginning its fifth decade, fans of both leagues hoped to see a new brand of baseball in the teens.

In fact, the new brand came in the form of a new ball itself from the Reach Company. Ben Shibe, who was also the namesake of the Athletics ballpark and the team's principal stockholder, had created a baseball with a rubberized cork center. The ball's unveiling came during the 1910 World Series. Oddly, the juiced-up ball didn't have an immediate effect: only one homer was hit in the 5-game series. But after the American League began regular use of the newfangled ball in 1911, the National League followed with a similar sphere created by Spalding, its official supplier.

What followed was a brief but distinct surge in offense. Cub Heinie Zimmerman became the National League's first Triple Crown winner of the twentieth century, with marks of .372, 14 home runs, and 103 RBI. In 1911, teammate Frank "Wildfire" Schulte clubbed a loop-leading 21 homers. By 1913, however, both pitchers and defenses adjusted to the "lively" ball, and batting averages began to recede again.

The new ball might have stolen the thunder of Tyrus Raymond Cobb, who batted .420 in 1911 and .410 in 1912. For the decade, "The Georgia Peach" racked up a .387 average. Cobb had earned his first batting title with a .350 average as a twenty-year-old, three-year veteran of the Tigers; his 1907 title coincided with his team's pennant.

In 1910, Cobb's average was thought to be .385, garnering a fourth straight batting title. By comparison, Cleveland's Napoleon Lajoie finished at .384, despite notching 6 straight hits against St. Louis on the last day of the season. (According to baseball lore, St. Louis Browns manager Jack O'Connor, simply to rile Cobb, ordered the third baseman to play deep against the speedy Lajoie, guaranteeing 7 straight bunt singles.)

OPPOSITE: *Far from being a boyhood idol or a media favorite, Ty Cobb turned baseball diamonds into battlegrounds and opponents into enemies. Cobb's "Georgia Peach" nickname reflected his birthplace, not his temperament.*

The batting race acquired new meaning when the Chalmers Motor Company offered a new automobile to each league's leading hitter. This gift, which was awarded for four seasons, encouraged the eventual adoption of the league naming Most Valuable Players. But in 1910, it only encouraged the heated rivalry between Cobb and Lajoie. Both men received cars that year, appeasing the pair but provoking decades of debate. It was more than a half-century later when research finally proved that a scorer mistakenly counted one of Cobb's hits twice, meaning that Lajoie should have owned the batting title outright.

In 1910, president William Howard Taft was the first to bless the game officially by throwing out the ceremonial first pitch at the season opener. From a flag-draped box on the first baseline of Washington's National Park, Senators pitcher Walter "The Big Train" Johnson was the lucky receiver in the group that assembled to compete for the pomp and circumstance pitch.

The Chicago White Stockings claimed the honor of presenting the decade's first new stadium, Comiskey Park. Built on the site of a former city dump, the south-side home held 28,800 fans after the team moved there on July 1, 1910.

But it was Chicago's National Leaguers who hosted a World Series that year. The Cubs double-play combination of shortstop Joe Tinker, second baseman Johnny Evers, and first sacker Frank Chance was immortalized in

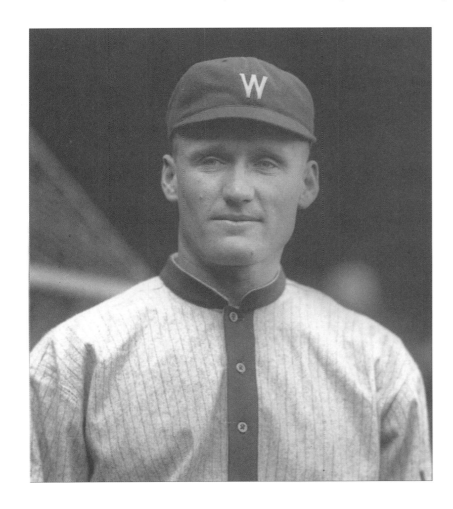

LEFT, TOP: *Having a team in Washington, D.C., allowed many a president to hurl a ceremonial first pitch, christening the new season. William Howard Taft was the first leader to embrace the ritual. The wary on-field spectators feared either the wrath of pushy photographers or a portly politician's errant throw.*

LEFT, BOTTOM: *Pitcher Walter Johnson, recipient of the president's pitch, didn't belong to a perennial contender. Nevertheless, the tireless Senators pitcher was one of baseball's greatest winners in the 1910s.*

this ditty by Franklin P. Adams in the 1910 *New York Mail*:

> These are the saddest of possible words—
> Tinker to Evers to Chance.
> Trio of Bear Cubs and fleeter than birds—
> Tinker to Evers to Chance.
> Ruthlessly pricking our gonfalon bubble,
> Making a Giant hit into a double,
>> Words that are weighty with nothing but
>> trouble,
>> Tinkers to Evers to Chance.

Without a single poem to their credit, the Philadelphia Athletics drubbed the Cubs in a 5-game World Series. Despite the ode to Chicago's fielding, the team committed a dozen errors during those games.

Pitcher Jack Coombs, who contributed 3 complete-game wins to the Philly effort, was one of the buried treasures that Athletics manager Connie Mack had mined from America's college campuses. Coombs, fresh from Colby College in Maine, set an AL record in 1906 with a 24-inning complete game. In 1910, his 13 shutouts became another league mark.

Another of Mack's finest collegiate finds was Eddie Collins. A varsity quarterback at Columbia University, he played part-time under the assumed name of Sullivan for Philadelphia in 1906–1907 to maintain his amateur athletic status for college football. Part of Mack's "$100,000 infield," Collins helped the Athletics to a fourth pennant in five years in 1914, becoming the league's Most Valuable Player. His reward was being sold to the White Sox in one of Mack's periodic personnel purges to cut the payroll.

For the first half of the 1910s, the Athletics were the American League's team to beat, while Cobb was the player to be stopped both on and off the field. On May 15, 1912, Cobb waded into the stands of Hilltop Park to pummel Highlanders fan Claude Lueker, a heckler heard to call the star a "half-nigger." The battle was one-sided, considering that Lueker had only one hand.

Cobb was suspended, and his Tigers teammates went on strike three days later. Baseball saw its first strike-breaking replacement players, a ragtag bunch that included a religion student named Aloysius Travers. The future priest tossed a complete game, but was defrocked by a 24–2 margin. Travers' battery mate was Deacon McGuire, a

LEFT: *Baseball began the teens on a tragic note, losing star Cleveland hurler Addie Joss to meningitis at age thirty-one. The four-time 20-game winner's funeral wasn't during an off-day for his teammates, a dilemma that caused a near-strike. Billy Sunday gave the eulogy at Joss' funeral.*

forty-eight-year-old coach. The elder receiver did contribute a single and a run scored, though. After a 1-game impasse, all the legitimate Tigers paid token fines and returned to the field. Cobb's penalty was a $50 fine.

Baseball's second season in the teens was delayed for a fallen hero. Cleveland hurler Addie Joss reported for spring training in 1911, but fell ill on April 3. Tubercular meningitis claimed the thirty-one-year-old's life eleven days later. He had hidden his illness from the public, even from teammates. In fact, Joss had spun his second career no-hitter just one year earlier before ending his 1910 campaign on July 25 with a sore arm. Joss had debuted with the Blues (now the Indians) in 1902, launching his big-league career with a 1-hitter. His lifetime 160–97 record included a 1.88 ERA, the second finest in baseball history.

Joss may have been one of baseball's first players-turned-announcers. From 1907 through 1909, he spent off-seasons covering sports for newspapers in Toledo and Cleveland, reporting on the World Series and other events.

To attend Joss' funeral, his teammates vowed to skip the next-day game in Detroit. Fearing that management wouldn't grant a day off, the players simply didn't show up, postponing the season opener. Cleveland Naps owner Charles W. Somers talked AL boss Ban Johnson out of threatening players back to the diamond, and later that year, the

BELOW: *Baseball began updating its arenas in the teens, including a facelift for the Polo Grounds in 1911. The wooden ballparks were constant fire hazards, and some simply couldn't serve the mushrooming crowds throughout the era.*

Naps played an exhibition game against an all-star team, raising $13,000 for the Joss family. Despite public approval of the cause and concept, baseball wouldn't revive the all-star game concept for two more decades.

Baseball owners agreed on one concept in the teens—that of creating unique, permanent homes for teams. After the auspicious addition of Comiskey Park, baseball eliminated its collection of outdated wooden relics with diamond showcases that would become traditions for nearly a half-century. New York received the new Polo Grounds in 1911. In 1912, Boston Red Sox fans welcomed Fenway Park, and Cincinnati rebuilt burnt-down Crosley Field. Brooklyn created Ebbets Field in 1913, and Detroit got Navin Field (later to become Tiger Stadium). Boston's NL relatives built Braves Field in 1915. The new Beantown structure housed forty thousand compared to Fenway's thirty-five thousand.

One stadium housed baseball in New York in 1913. The refurbished Polo

Grounds gained a second team when the Highlanders abandoned Hilltop Park and their old name to become the Yankees, roommates of the New York Giants.

The Giants' 103–48 record took the NL pennant in 1912, outdistancing the second-place Pirates by 10 games. Opposing Boston in the World Series, a rare eighth game was played when the second contest was called because of darkness. Host Boston was blessed by a dropped fly ball by center fielder Fred Snodgrass to begin the bottom of the tenth in that eighth game.

Fred Merkle, whose base-running "boner" had cost the Giants a 1908 pennant against the Cubs, singled the go-ahead run in the tenth, creating an assumption of victory. Yet Merkle's potential game-winner has been overshadowed by history's rush to celebrate his "$30,000 Muff." (Cynical scribes noted the amount as the difference between the winning and losing team's Series share.) It happened after the Snodgrass error put a runner on second and Christy Mathewson dished up a walk: Tris Speaker lofted a foul fly that first baseman Merkle didn't bother to chase. His failure to act gave Speaker second life to single in the tying run and eventually win the decisive game, 3–2.

But true ballplayers remember that the playing is more important than the pennant. Before his death in 1974, Snodgrass philosophized: "My years in baseball had their ups and downs, their strike and their torment. But the years I look back at most fondly, and those I'd like

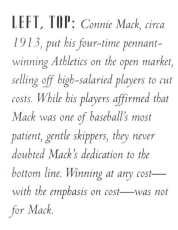

LEFT, TOP: *Connie Mack, circa 1913, put his four-time pennant-winning Athletics on the open market, selling off high-salaried players to cut costs. While his players affirmed that Mack was one of baseball's most patient, gentle skippers, they never doubted Mack's dedication to the bottom line. Winning at any cost—with the emphasis on cost—was not for Mack.*

LEFT, BOTTOM: *Fred Merkle avenged his 1908 baserunning "bonehead" blunder with a decade of speed unprecedented for a six-foot-one-inch 190-pounder. He recorded eight years of 20 or more steals, and a career-high 49 stolen bases in 1911.*

RIGHT: *Tris Speaker, shown here before a 1910 matchup, sparked the Red Sox to World Series titles in 1912 and 1915, providing sterling defense in center field. He joined the Indians in 1916, becoming player-manager in 1919.*

ABOVE: *Five-foot-five-inch shortstop Walter Maranville was nicknamed "Rabbit" because of his size and speed. His input helped the 1914 Boston Braves achieve a 4-game sweeping upset in World Series play against the much-heralded Philadelphia Athletics.*

most to live over, are the years when I was playing center field for the New York Giants."

Boston was the site of two World Series dramas during the early teens. In 1914, the NL club was heralded as the "Miracle Braves." The team had been mired in last place on July 4 in part because of losing 18 of its first 22 games. Yet the Braves sewed up the pennant against the Giants by a 10½-game margin, losing only 10 of their last 44 games.

For the first time ever, the World Series featured a 4-game sweep. The once-mighty Athletics were the victims, leading owner-manager Mack to

gut the roster before the 1915 season began, selling or trading once-untouchable stars. And though the sweep ended in Boston, the Braves didn't even accomplish the win in their home park. Instead of using the small, deteriorating South End Grounds, they accepted the Red Sox offer to use the newer, larger Fenway Park for the postseason.

Walter "Rabbit" Maranville was at the heart of the Braves' success. The five-foot-five-inch shortstop led the league in five fielding categories, then batted .308 in postseason play. His nickname was due to his size and perpetual motion, and was

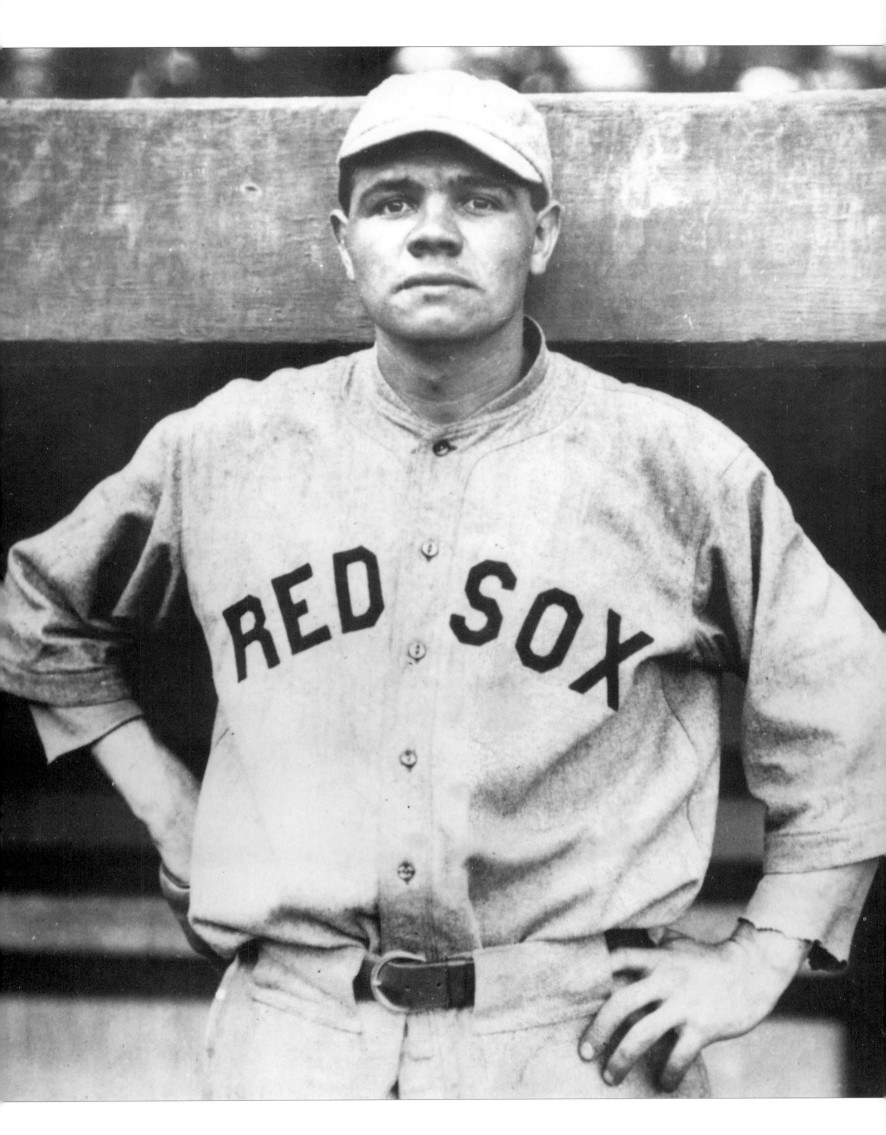

OPPOSITE: *Pitcher George Herman Ruth provided the Red Sox with 18 wins in his 1915 rookie season. A year earlier, Boston nearly lost the "Babe" to the Cincinnati Red Stockings on waivers amid his minor league demotion.*

ABOVE, LEFT: *The gleaming spikes of Tyrus Raymond Cobb became a familiar sight on base paths during the teens. The Detroit speedster became the decade's stolen base authority while provoking numerous confrontations with opposing infielders.*

ABOVE, RIGHT: *Cobb seemed immortal at bat, though his speed and daring in center field didn't come without risk. He made 144 errors in the 1910s, attempting many seemingly impossible plays. Of course, his battles with writers didn't win sympathy from official scorer/reporters, who assigned errors.*

supposedly created by a seven-year-old fan during Maranville's 1912 rookie season.

In his never-completed autobiography (which was published by the Society for American Baseball Research [SABR] in 1991), Maranville recalled the beginnings of the miracle season: "When we got back east they started calling us Misfits, Country Buttered Ball Tossers, and whatnot. With all this, [George] Stallings, our manager, kept encouraging us by saying, 'Stick in there; we will show them.'"

The Red Sox showed the American League—and baseball—when it gained a left-handed pitcher named George Herman Ruth in 1914. He collected a 2–1 record and 3.91 ERA in four appearances. In 1915, his first full year, the twenty-year-old "Babe" went 18–8. More important, the six-foot-two-inch, 190-pounder hit .315 with a team-leading 4 homers and 21 RBI.

Ruth spent the majority of 1914 as a minor leaguer with Providence of the International League. To send Ruth down, Boston had to get waivers cleared on its prospect. Cincinnati put in a claim, which AL president Ban Johnson begged to be removed. Cincy owner Garry Herrmann, the former National Commission leader from the early 1900s, finally backed down.

In 1914, for the first time in baseball history, the National and American Leagues found a common cause to fight when the Federal League fielded eight teams, too. Most were in big cities: St. Louis, Brooklyn, Pittsburgh, Chicago, Kansas City, Baltimore, and Buffalo. The Indianapolis charter club was replaced in 1915 with Newark. Players great and small were tempted: even Cobb threatened to "jump," but Detroit ponied up enough funds to make him baseball's highest-paid player.

One star who switched to the Federal League was Joe Tinker, who served as a player-manager. He skippered a second-place entry in 1914 and was a 1915 pennant winner. Weeghman Park was built to house Chicago's Federal League entry. Later, the ballpark would become Wrigley Field.

Fueling the Federal League's birth was the Fraternity of Professional Base Ball Players, a union formed after the panic over the Joss death. The pitcher's family was left in debt, prompting other players to consider their own financial futures. Ultimately, the National and American Leagues made only temporary concessions to players, and those were made only while the Federal League existed. The third league ceased after 1915, after unsuccessfully attempting to repeal baseball's antitrust exemption. Kenesaw Mountain Landis was the

RIGHT: *Cobb served as a U.S. Army captain in 1917. Despite the commission, he managed to play 152 games that year. Furthermore, the military honor brought a rare bit of positive attention to Cobb's constant controversies.*

ABOVE: *The 1917 White Sox wore army uniforms for an on-field pregame drill. World War I's threat to the nation gave teams the chance to erase their sometimes mercenary images by displaying patriotism and community loyalty.*

ruling judge in the case, his first case in a long association with the sport.

Like their major league comrades, Federal League players received no lasting benefits, but the owners didn't come away empty-handed. The court settlement allowed partial ownership of major league teams, including a controlling interest in the St. Louis Browns. Players still in the majors saw their union crumble. Salaries were slashed and hopes were dashed.

The only lasting lesson for major league owners from the Federal League aftermath was that fans couldn't be taken for granted. Fans had been wooed by the Federal League, and if caution was not exercised, they could be lured again. So change began: in 1917, the St. Louis Cardinals pioneered the "knothole gang" program to provide free tickets to underprivileged boys. A year earlier, the Cubs were the first team to allow fans to keep foul balls that were hit into the stands. From 1911 through 1917, the Cardinals were headed by baseball's first female owner, Helene Robison Britton.

But it was the heroes who kept the fans' romance alive. Charles M. Conlon was one of the decade's on-field heroes, yet many fans have never heard his name. Without wielding a bat or glove, Conlon bestowed fame on numerous players and teams with his groundbreaking photographs. He began photographing baseball in 1906 for the New York *World Telegram* newspaper, and his shots later appeared in such newspapers as the *Spalding Guide* and *The Sporting News*, helping to redefine how fans remembered the sport. Long before videotape or scoreboard instant replays, getting a next-day look on the sports page was the next best thing. Photographers in the teens bravely camped only yards behind first or third base—even hunkering near the on-deck circle—to gain the best vantage points.

Conlon was one of the first to pioneer the technology of action photography, and his masterpiece is probably a 1909 shot of a sneering, spikes-high Ty Cobb. Cobb's savage slide upended New York Highlanders third baseman Jimmy Austin into a cloud of dirt. When the shot was finally published in the 1912 *Spalding Guide*, an anonymous editor sketched in a crude blob to represent the baseball, which had actually sailed past third into left field because of a catcher's throwing error.

Baseball-related novels drew a huge following, starting with the 1912 ghost-written *Pitching in a Pinch*, by Christy Mathewson. Though it was fiction and, at the least, cowritten, the book did offer a true "inside" glimpse of life as a big leaguer.

While the 1919 Chicago American Leaguers sported white hosiery, their dark finish amid the mob-controlled, gambling-tainted World Series would brand the team the "Black Sox." Actually, sportswriters considered the nickname earlier in the year, when protesting players paraded in dirty uniforms to protest owner Charles Comiskey's refusal to pay the team's laundry bills.

However, as World War I loomed, the song was welcomed with mass singing and applause. When theatrical Red Sox owner Harry Frazee's club returned for games in Boston, he ordered that the song open each game.

The eventful end of the teens is remembered mostly for a World Series tainted by gamblers' bribes: the Black Sox scandal. The cloud over the White Sox, although not revealed for more than a year, still hangs over baseball's accomplishments from 1919.

That year Boston benefitted from Ruth's record 29 home runs, but wound up in sixth place with a 66–71 record. Walter Johnson pitched to a 20–14 mark with an AL-finest 1.49 ERA, despite the Senators' seventh-place 56–84 floundering. Cobb continued to add to his collection of batting crowns, swatting .384.

White Sox pitcher Ed Cicotte was the league's leader in complete games (30) and victories (29). His win total bested the 28 triumphs he posted during the team's world championship campaign. Legend has it that cheapskate owner Charles Comiskey benched the hurler at season's end to prevent him from winning 30 and earning a $10,000 contract incentive. Such tightfistedness was nothing new: in 1918, team members chose to wear dirty uniforms for weeks to protest Comiskey's refusal to pay their laundry bills. Hence, the nickname came from their appearance instead of from their corruption.

Joseph Jefferson Jackson had paced the ChiSox during the regular season, with 7 homers, 96 RBI, and a .351 average. "Shoeless Joe" was legendary for playing in socks only, as a minor leaguer with ill-fitting shoes. Following his debut with the 1908 Athletics, the former millworker tallied a .408 for

Fans wanted immediate information on their favorite teams, and at this point, the sport still had no radio coverage. When public interest peaked around World Series time, newspapers would post huge scoreboards outside their offices. Some newspapers would simply count runs scored per inning. More ornate setups would re-create diamonds, enabling the wire service ticker to give a batter-by-batter summary. Methodically, spotters would post names on appropriate bases, simulating every run scored. Even without offering a single picture of the real game or any detailed descriptions, the boards attracted hundreds of fans who crowded streets and sidewalks to stare, cheer, and boo as if they were box-seat holders at the stadium.

Although the histories of the Cubs and the World Series are not subjects that have gone hand in hand, the team did manage to spark a tradition while hosting the first game of the 1918 Fall Classic. During the seventh-inning stretch, the band in attendance struck up "The Star-Spangled Banner," which would one day be adopted as the country's national anthem.

the 1911 Indians, the only player besides Cobb to exceed the hallowed .400 mark that decade.

Promised $20,000 for his part in the fix against Cincinnati, Jackson actually received only $5,000. However, questions remain over how serious he was about throwing any games. His .375 Series average and 12 hits led both teams, and

Jackson's home run was the only four-bagger by anyone in 8 games.

Few silver linings were found in baseball in 1919. That year's biggest dividend would not pay off for years, but the payoff wouldn't be forgotten. Jackie Robinson, baseball's future desegregationist, was born in Cairo, Georgia.

Outfielder Joe Jackson coped with illiteracy throughout his checkered career. The South Carolina native's alleged participation in the betting scandal overshadowed his stellar postseason hitting. Despite legend, no confirmation was ever made of the young fan who supposedly exclaimed, "Say it ain't so, Joe."

CHAPTER FOUR

1920-1929

Before 1920, many men had been anointed with the title "Father of Baseball." Soon, baseball would have its first king.

Owners panicked as word spread that the 1919 World Series was purposely lost by eight White Sox players on the take. Hugh Fullerton, the dean of Chicago baseball reporters, was among the first to speculate on the possibilities of a fix. Once-great pitcher and ex–Reds manager Christy Mathewson made similar observations while covering the Series for a press syndicate.

Kenesaw Mountain Landis, a federal judge appointed in 1905 by President Theodore Roosevelt, was no stranger to the game. He had ruled in favor of the established leagues in the 1916 Federal League monopoly lawsuit, leading to speculation that he was owed the appointment of commissioner by team owners.

However, Judge Landis (who insisted on retaining his title) wanted no ceremonial post, even at $50,000 per year. He wanted to be baseball's judge and jury, with none of his decisions to face appeal.

Landis waited for a Chicago grand jury to convene on September 22, 1920. Historians falsely assume the investigation was limited to, and inspired by, the 1919 Series. On the contrary, a string of gambling-related incidents surrounding the majors led to the hearings. Mathewson, as then–Cincinnati manager, suspended first baseman "Prince" Hal Chase on July 25, 1918, after suspecting that he was throwing games. Suspected of being involved with Chase, Lee Magee was swapped to the Cubs, only to be released.

Magee sued the Cubs for back salary. Although he lost, the court action revealed details of Magee's shenanigans with Chase, confirming the worst suspicions. The Cubs suffered another moral blot in August 1920, when newspapers reported that pitcher Claude Hendrix was benched for accepting a bribe to lose.

OPPOSITE: *Judge Kenesaw Mountain Landis, baseball's first commissioner, got his name from Kenesaw Mountain, Georgia, the site of a Civil War battle where his father was wounded. He began more than two decades of iron-fisted rule on November 12, 1920, bent on removing all hints of gambling from the game. For more than one year, he retained his federal judgeship while overseeing professional baseball.*

At the end of the eight-day proceedings, pitcher Ed Cicotte and outfielder Joe Jackson confessed to the assistant state's attorney that they had taken money to lose the Series, linking teammates Fred McMullin, "Swede" Risberg, Lefty Williams, Buck Weaver, Hap Felsch, and Chick Gandil in the crime. Team owner Charles Comiskey, who had denied all rumors a year earlier, promptly ignored his club's second-place standing and suspended the group.

The infamous eight stood trial, and all were acquitted. Transcripts of Cicotte's and Jackson's testimonies disappeared, and the bunch was dismissed for lack of evidence. In their favor, Chicago's individual performances in 1920 seemed sincere and admirable: 20-win seasons from Williams and Cicotte, with 100-plus RBI from Felsch and Jackson.

Only one day after the verdict was announced, Judge Landis issued his own decree. Regardless of any court findings, the Chicago eight would be banned from professional baseball for life.

Throwing games seemed mild compared to the tragedy of August 16, 1920, at the Polo Grounds. The Yankees started Carl Mays, known for his unorthodox submarine delivery. (A year earlier, Mays had been traded from Boston to New York for $40,000 and two players. Because

LEFT: *In this photograph taken on September 23, 1920, White Sox owner Charles Comiskey seems to be a passive observer in the trial of his eight players. Comiskey escaped legal tangles and public wrath by underpaying the players accused of taking bribes. However, Comiskey's ravaged team enjoyed only one contending season before his death in 1931.*

BELOW: *Illinois assistant state attorney Hartley Replogle (left) shown here with Ring Lardner, was among the first to hear Joe Jackson describe how he accepted a $5,000 bribe from gamblers to fix the 1919 World Series. Jackson was promised $20,000 but never saw the whole payment.*

ABOVE: *Yankees owner Jacob Ruppert (seated, right) watches his star acquisition, Babe Ruth, sign a contract. Although Ruth threw left-handed, his turn-of-the-century upbringing had encouraged him to write with his right hand.*

BELOW: *Cleveland infielder Ray Chapman would become baseball's first on-field fatality on August 16, 1920, when he was struck in the head by a pitch from Yankee Carl Mays. Ironically, the pitch wasn't that wild; Chapman was famed for crowding the plate. He died twelve hours later.*

RIGHT: *In 1919, Carl Mays was an accomplished moundsman with a 26–11 record in 1920. A five-time 20-game winner with 208 career victories, Mays had to live with being linked to baseball tragedy until his death in 1971.*

Mays had gone AWOL from the Red Sox ten days before the deal, AL president Ban Johnson wanted Mays suspended and the deal canceled. The Yankees went to court to prevent Johnson from interfering.)

That day, Mays hit Cleveland Indians shortstop Ray Chapman in the head with a pitch. The batter died the next morning from a skull fracture. In spite of the circumstances, Johnson bore no grudge against Mays, and found the pitcher innocent of wrongdoing after a weeklong investigation.

Mays was only the first Boston player to be piece-mealed out to the rival Yankees. The most famous player would be sold in January 1920, when Red Sox owner Harry Harrison Frazee needed money to bankroll theatrical ventures. Because Frazee's first love was the stage, he sold Babe Ruth for $125,000. Later, however, the meat of the deal was revealed: the Yankees ownership included a 300,000 loan, with Fenway Park put up as Frazee's collateral.

Did New York see an immediate payoff in its investment? In the standings, Ruth's dynamite bat powered the Yanks to a mere third-place finish, despite a record 54 home runs to complement 137 RBI and a .376 average. Even with 95 wins, the Yankees missed a pennant by a slim 3 games.

Without the Babe, the first World Series of the 1920s would be remembered as a competition between two "grandfathers."

In order to rid the post–Black Sox baseball world of all traces of scandal, a postseason 1920 rule stated that the spitball and other unorthodox deliveries were to be abolished. Special exception was made to allow each team to name two pitchers as spitball pitchers for the 1921 season; thereafter, no spitballers would be allowed.

In keeping with this grandfather clause, which allowed veteran deceivers to remain in the game, the Cleveland Indians kept Stan Coveleski on the list. Born Stanley Anthony Kowalewski, the right-hander had an elder brother, Harry, who had started pitching with the 1907 Phillies. Stan, the alum-sucking spitballer, once said: "Sometimes I'd go maybe 2 or 3 innings without throwing one. But I'd always have them looking for it."

Brooklyn's Burleigh Grimes, the ace of the Robins staff, chewed slippery elm to create his wet wonders. Because the chew irritated the skin on his face, the hurler wouldn't shave on days he pitched. This earned him the nickname "Ol' Stubblebeard." Grimes ended the twenties with 190 victories, more than any hurler in that decade. Perhaps Grimes was summing up his spitball philosophy when he said, "I've always contended that baseball is made up of very few big and dramatic moments, but rather it's a beautifully put-together pattern of countless little subtleties that finally add up to the big moment."

LEFT: *Stanley "Bucky" Harris defied all baseball odds. In his first season as manager of a perennial cellar dweller, the twenty-seven-year-old second baseman won it all in 1924. He coached the Washington Senators (for whom he also played) into world champions. All this came from a fellow who dropped out of school at age thirteen, playing ball when he wasn't mining coal.*

BELOW: *Before the second game of the 1926 World Series, Rogers Hornsby grabbed some batting practice. A fill-in manager for skipper John McGraw, Hornsby lasted only one year with the New York Giants. Despite managerial savvy and a potent bat, Hornsby's bombastic personality was more than many owners could stomach.*

In the postseason matchup, Cleveland won 5 out of 7. Coveleski yielded only 5 hits per outing in 3 complete-game victories. The fifth game featured three milestones: Cleveland's Elmer Smith hit the first grand slam in Series history; teammate Jim Bagby was the first pitcher to homer in a Series; and as a finale, second baseman Bill Wambsganss pulled off the first unassisted triple play in the postseason.

For the next three years, New York clubs would rule Series play. The Yankees met their landlords, the Giants, in the 1921 event. All 8 games would be played at the Polo Grounds, still sizzling from Ruth's new regular-season record of 59 homers. John McGraw's National Leaguers prevailed, while holding the Babe to one bases-empty homer in Game Four, the only Yankee dinger of the Series.

During the off-season, Ruth ballooned to 240 pounds. He flaunted a rule that stated that no World Series participants could play in off-season exhibitions. Judge Landis suspended Ruth for the first six weeks of 1922. Some worried that the baseball dictator would sit the Bambino down for the whole season. Nonetheless, the late start was of little consequence to Ruth. He finished with 35 round-trippers, only 4 behind St. Louis Browns league leader Ken Williams.

The Giants not only repeated as champions, but they swept the Yankees in 4 straight. Ruth was limited to a single, a double, and 1 RBI in 17 plate appearances.

The 1921 Pirates, at 90–63, missed the pennant by only 4 games. During an August 5 home game at Forbes Field against Philadelphia, Pittsburgh radio station KDKA featured Harold Arlin airing the first-ever major league broadcast.

Arlin was a twenty-six-year-old announcer from Illinois. "Frankly, we didn't know what the reaction would be, whether we'd be talking into a total vacuum or whether somebody would actually hear us," he recalled years later. Nearly two decades would pass before all teams would take radio seriously, quelling fears that "free" games on radio would stop fans from buying tickets.

In 1922, no NL team had displayed any near-Ruthian sluggers. Finally, the Cardinals—despite tying for third place behind the Giants—offered a royal substitute.

Rogers "Rajah" Hornsby debuted with St. Louis in 1915, but didn't reach double digits in homers until he socked 21 in 1921. Hornsby won the 1922 Triple Crown, when he batted .401 with 42 homers and 152 RBI, while leading the senior circuit in eight different categories. Seven times in the 1920s he would win league batting crowns, including two more years hitting over the .400 plateau.

The Yankees were the talk of baseball in 1923, even before the season started. In less than one year, Yankee Stadium, the "House That Ruth Built," had been completed. The mammoth park hosted an inaugural crowd of fifty-eight thousand, though actual attendance, including those outside the stadium, was estimated at 74,127. The Yankees downed the Red Sox, 4–1.

The following year, New York's ownership of the world title was halted by the most unlikely of foes: the 1924 Washington Senators.

"Baseball is simply a dramatization of the life struggle of man," pitcher Walter Johnson once said. Johnson's career mirrored his philosophy. The Kansas native began with the Washington Senators in 1907. Although Johnson earned his eleventh 20-win season in 1924, the team had never before reached the postseason.

Second baseman Bucky Harris, at age twenty-seven, was named the team's player-manager. Johnson's eighteen-year wait for a World Series crown, along with the rise of the "Boy Wonder" skipper, made the underdog Senators a sentimental favorite.

Johnson earned only 1 victory in Washington's championship, but it was the one that mattered. Johnson's 2 starts resulted in 2 losses. For the seventh game, "The Big Train" relieved Fred "Firpo" Marberry to start the ninth inning. With the score knotted at 3-all, his 4 shutout innings paved the way for the win.

Back in New York, what seemed like a permanent fixture was installed at Yankee Stadium. "The Iron Horse," known officially as Henry Louis Gehrig, took up residence at first base. Born Ludwig Heinrich Gehrig, he was plucked from the Columbia University team as a freshman. Although he saw only spotty action in his first two years in the majors (24 games spread over 1923–1924), Gehrig became the team's steady first sacker on June 1, 1925, his first week of playing in 2,130 consecutive games.

Gehrig took over first base from Wally Pipp, a thirty-two-year-old veteran who had been a Yankees regular since 1915. Pipp was a two-time home run champion, leading the American League with totals of 12 and 9, in 1916 and 1917, respectively. In 1924, his 19 triples were another league best.

According to myth, Pipp was a hypochondriac, fussing about a headache, which led to Gehrig's chance to work every day. In truth, Pipp was bonked in the head during batting practice, and that helped Gehrig to win the spot. Regardless, Pipp was sold to Cincinnati on February 1, 1926, for $7,500. Three seasons later, he was out of base-

ball. Today, the term "Wally Pipp" is a media buzzword for any injured player who is overshadowed by his replacement.

The 1925 pennant belonged to the Senators for a second straight year. They defended their league title by an 8½-game margin. The team had added Coveleski and Johnson, a pair of 20-game winners who they had obtained from the Indians.

Pittsburgh, the Senator's 1925 Series opponents, exhibited two of the fastest outfielders in baseball, Hazen "KiKi" Cuyler and Max Carey. In the NL stolen base race, Carey and Cuyler finished first and second, with totals of 46 and 41, respectively.

Defense outranked speed as a deciding factor for the victorious Pirates in the 1925 Fall Classic. Washington's shortstop Roger Peckinpaugh was charged with 8 errors in 7 games, constituting a dubious postseason record. Incredible as it may seem, Peckinpaugh had been named the league's MVP prior to the Series.

In 1926, the St. Louis Cardinals emerged as a new NL force. General manager Wesley Branch Rickey had orchestrated the team's resurgence by creating the first farm system when he became president and team manager in 1919. Rickey crafted a web of minor league teams, all St. Louis—owned, to de-

velop future Cardinals and surplus talent ready to sell to other franchises.

Skeptical sportswriters dubbed Rickey "The Mahatma" for his mystical persona. He restored St. Louis financially by squeezing player salaries, while speaking endlessly on moral virtues. He never swore beyond the exclamation "Judas Priest!" and claimed that he upheld a youthful promise to his mother to keep the Sabbath holy by avoiding Sunday baseball.

Although Rickey retained his front-office throne, Hornsby became the new field boss for the 1926 Redbirds. Besides managing the club to an 89–65 finish, he hit .317 with 11 homers and 93 RBI.

Hornsby's wisest move of the year may have been his encouraging the team to sign thirty-nine-year-old pitcher Grover Cleveland Alexander, who was waived in midseason by the Cubs. Known as "Old Pete," the hurler suffered from alcoholism, epilepsy, and hearing loss from serving in World War I.

Alexander worked more than 200 innings in adding 9 wins to the St. Louis pennant drive. In the Series, he sparkled in Game Two. His complete-game 4-hitter included 10 strikeouts.

Alexander's star would shine again in the seventh game. The Yankees loaded the bases in the bottom of the seventh. With two outs, Hornsby summoned the allegedly hungover Alexander. Following a 1–1 count, Tony Lazzeri smashed the next serving into left field, going foul by inches. A final

ABOVE: *Washington shortstop Roger Peckinpaugh (left) wishes good luck to Pittsburgh opponent Max Carey prior to the start of the 1926 World Series. Carey was indeed the luckier of the pair, enjoying a .458 average as his Pirates claimed a 7-game championship.*

RIGHT: *More than a decade before he began his cigar-chomping role as general manager of the Brooklyn Dodgers, Branch Rickey helped build the St. Louis Cardinals into a perpetual winner. Through Rickey, the Cards developed an unmatched "farm system" of minor league teams. The former catcher stepped down as St. Louis field manager after the 1925 season, having never finished higher than third place.*

The 1927 New York Yankees "Murderer's Row" featured (from left to right) Earle Combs, Bob Meusel, Lou Gehrig, and Babe Ruth. The grim looks from this September photograph do not reflect that the four Yanks were in the midst of cruising to a 110-win season while winning the pennant by a 19-game margin.

curveball enticed a swing and a miss. Two more scoreless innings would preserve a 3–2 lead and the reputation of a faded hero.

Baseball suffered a strange loss after the 1926 season. Player-managers Tris Speaker and Ty Cobb left the game unexpectedly. Retired pitcher Dutch Leonard claimed he had proof that Cobb, Speaker, and retired pitcher Smokey Joe Wood conspired with him to bet on a rigged game that had been held before the infamous fixed World Series.

AL president Johnson told the pair to leave the game to avoid another gambling inquisition. Johnson had paid Leonard $20,000 to keep quiet with his charges. Commissioner Landis would rule that Leonard's old letters, which supposedly proved mass guilt, were misunderstood. No action would be taken against either player. However, the power struggle would bring about Johnson's forced resignation in July 1927.

Forgiven, Cobb would spend his last two seasons, 1927 and 1928, with the Athletics. Speaker would never manage again but would spend 1927 as a Senators regular, and his 1928 swan song would be as Cobb's unlikely part-time teammate.

The Yankees earned the billing "Murderer's Row" in 1927 for their 110 victories and 158 home runs. Leading the long-ball parade were 60 homers by Ruth and 47 four-baggers from Gehrig. The New York power factory, however, generated only 2 Ruth blasts in its 4-game Series sweep of Pittsburgh.

The opposing Pirates entered the postseason with their own nickname parade. Brothers Paul and Lloyd Waner were christened "Big Poison" and "Little Poison." Lloyd manned center field with Paul in right. Unlike the Yankees musclemen, neither Waner was physically intimidating. Paul was five feet eight and a half inches and 153 pounds while Lloyd was five feet eight inches and 150 pounds.

Although Paul's "Big" tag was given because he was exactly two years and eleven months older than Lloyd, the handles could also suggest their 1927 output. Paul's regular season statistics included 9 homers, 31 RBI, and a .380 average. Lloyd added 223 hits (including a record-setting 198 singles) and a .355 mark.

How did the Pirates get two brothers in one outfield? After Paul joined Pittsburgh in 1926, he lobbied for his brother's signing, telling team brass, "He's a better player than me."

The Cardinals and the Yankees made the 1928 World Series into a rematch of the 1926 contest. New York avenged the prior upset with a 4-game romp. Gehrig tied a 1926 Ruth record with 4 home runs. Ruth's new marks included 10 hits and 9 runs scored.

Charles "Chick" Hafey had earned a starting outfield post with the 1927 Cards, responding

In perhaps one of the greatest one-on-one confrontations in World Series history, seemingly over-the-hill Cardinals hurler Grover Cleveland Alexander (below, left) bested Tony "Poosh 'Em Up" Lazzeri (below, right) with a seventh-inning strikeout in the climactic seventh game of the 1926 Fall Classic. The Yankees rookie struck out a league-leading 96 times during the regular season. Although Lazzeri was on his way to a fourteen-year career, "Ol' Pete" saw his pitching career end after 9 games for the 1930 Pirates.

Oklahoma-born Lloyd "Little Poison" Waner played outfield for the Pirates along with his brother. Lloyd debuted with Pittsburgh in 1927, the year of his only World Series. Lloyd wowed the National League as a speedy lead-off hitter, accumulating just 173 strike-outs in his eighteen big-league seasons.

with a .329 batting average and league-best .590 slugging percentage. His blossoming career seemed at risk in 1929, however, when a sinus infection threatened his eyesight. He started to wear eyeglasses, which were still a rarity for players. Baseball was stunned by a bespectacled batsman, especially one who wove perennial .300-plus years and a 1931 batting crown.

Just when "dynasty" labels were being readied for the Cards and the Yanks, two upstart clubs became the stars of 1929. Through 1928, four NL clubs—Chicago, Boston, Philadelphia, and Cincinnati—had gone without pennants in the decade. Four AL squads—the Browns, White Sox, Tigers, and Athletics—faced the same drought.

Manager Joe McCarthy's Cubs missed the NL pennant by 4 games in 1928. A season later, their 98–54 record grabbed the flag by a 10-game margin. The addition of second baseman Hornsby pushed the club over the first-place hump. Acquired from Boston for five players and $200,000, the high-priced, much-traveled infielder paid off with marks of .380, 39 homers, and 149 RBI. He

knocked in 10 fewer runs than the league leader, teammate Lewis Robert "Hack" Wilson.

"I've never played drunk," the combative Wilson once remarked. "Hung over, yes, but never drunk."

The Athletics relied on catcher Mickey Cochrane. Known as "Black Mike" for his competitive fire, Cochrane became the American League's Most Valuable Player on the strength of his durability and defense. In 1929, he added 7 homers, 95 RBI, and a .331 average.

When the Athletics opened the 1929 Series, manager Mack chose not to go with team ace Lefty Grove. Instead, he chose a thirty-five-year-old journeyman hurler named Howard Ehmke. Ehmke's beginnings were traced back to the Federal League in 1915. Cochrane, in a book called *Baseball: A Fan's Game,* recalled the scene a decade later:

I was to catch the game, and even I didn't know that Howard was to start it. Everybody, fans, writers and players alike, thought Mr. Mack had Lefty Grove warming up under the stands.

"Is *he* going to pitch?" I asked Mr. Mack when Ehmke started his warm-up.

"Yes, Mickey, he is," said the kindly old gentleman, and then with a twinkle in his eye: "He is, if it's all right with you."

"If he's good enough for you, he's good enough for me," I replied.

Not only did Ehmke win, but his complete-game 8-hitter included a World Series record of 13 strikeouts. This was from a little-used pitcher who went 1–2 during the regular season, posting 20 Ks in a total of 11 games. As the A's downed the Cubs in a 5-game affair, the "Mackmen" displayed true teamwork. Four different pitchers owned 1 win each. Every starter but Cochrane drove in at least 1 run, although the catcher collected 7 bases on balls and a .400 average.

The World Series was being played amid an even bigger drama. The stock market plummeted in October 1929, culminating with the panicked October 29 mass sell-off known as "Black Monday." Still, attendance continued to climb in 1929, as evidenced by the Cubs' one million-plus attendance.

However, baseball was a business, and no business was immune from the economic plague sweeping the nation. In the upcoming years, The Great American Pastime faced the Great Depression.

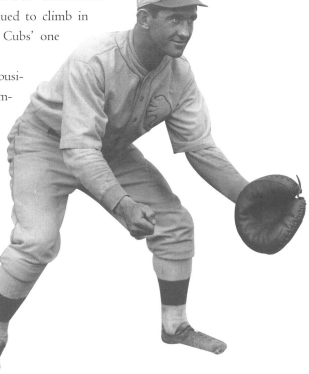

ABOVE: *Lou Gehrig, Tris Speaker, Ty Cobb, and Babe Ruth (left to right) assemble for a 1928 chat. Speaker and Cobb roamed the same outfield for the '28 Athletics in what proved to be the last season for both men. Speaker left the Indians and Cobb the Tigers after the 1926 season, when they were rumored (but never proven) to be involved in a betting scandal.*

RIGHT: *Pitcher Howard Ehmke appeared in only 11 games during the regular season for the 1929 Athletics. As a surprise starter to open the World Series, the right-hander did more than toss a complete-game win. His 13 strikeouts broke the record of Ed Walsh's dozen Ks in the 1906 Fall Classic. Here, Ehmke is shown warming up during 1928 spring training.*

CHAPTER FIVE

1930-1939

"**B**aseball is the greatest of all team sports."
President Herbert Hoover's praise of baseball might have been wishful think-ing for the country in 1930. In September of that year, unemployment fig-ures had reached five million. The figure had risen to nine million by October 1931. Compared to the bleak numbers facing the country's economy, baseball stats were welcomed news.

The consecutive-game streak on everyone's mind when the decade began be-longed not to a Yankee, but to a Cleveland Indian. Joe Sewell, the shortstop who had replaced Ray Chapman when he was killed by a pitch in 1920, finally took a breather in May 1930, following a streak of 1,102 consecutive games. Yet in the 109 games he played in that season, he endured only 3 strikeouts. In his fourteen-year career, Sewell fanned a mere 114 times. Where did such bat control come from? "When I was a boy," Sewell remembered, "I'd walk around with a pocket full of rocks or a Coca-Cola top and I can't remember not being able to hit them with a broomstick handle."

As hard times threatened attendance, teams everywhere struggled to keep the fans they had. The minor league ballpark in Des Moines, Iowa, was the site of the first permanent field lighting for night games in 1930. One by one, ballparks be-gan installing public address systems to replace the outdated tradition of mega-phone shouts from baseball's equivalent of town criers.

In the majors, games were marked by exploding offenses. Behind Hack Wil-son, the 90-win Cubs missed the Cardinals and the pennant by only 2 games. Their hard-drinking, hard-hitting outfielder soared with league marks of 56 home runs and 190 RBI to highlight a .356 average. Giants first baseman Bill Terry, at .401, became the last senior-circuit clouter to best .400 for more than a half-century. Yet few of the NL averages were that average in 1930. As a whole, the league batted .303. Contrastingly, the league's ERA was 4.97. The Brooklyn Robins' ERA, at 4.03, was an NL low.

ABOVE: *Joe Sewell began his career in 1920 as the infield replacement for Cleveland's Ray Chapman, who was killed by a pitched ball. Sewell concluded his career in 1933 as a Yankees third baseman. In the thirties, he struck out only 18 times over a four-year span.*

OPPOSITE: *President Herbert Hoover kicks off the 1931 season with a first pitch before the Washington Senators–Philadelphia Athletics matchup on April 14 as Washington manager Walter Johnson looks on. The Senators were on their way to a 92–62 season, which provided a third-place finish behind the pennant-winning A's. Both Hoover and Johnson would be seeking new jobs in 1932.*

The Athletics, with 102 wins, seemed unstoppable as defending world champions. However, no team found Yankees Gehrig and Ruth easy to stop. Ruth chalked up another homer title with 49, hitting .359 with 153 RBI. Gehrig was the AL king of RBI with 174, adding a .379 average and 41 home runs. However, the fireworks still couldn't carry New York past a third-place finish.

Philadelphia and the Cardinals battled in a 6-game World Series showdown. St. Louis managed 10 home runs and 3 more total hits than the A's, yet Connie Mack's club walked away the winners.

The following season, the Athletics and the Cards repeated their pennants. Philadelphia owned three 20-game winners, including league leader Lefty Grove, who had 31 victories. Left fielder Al Simmons, known as "Bucketfoot" for his odd stride away from the plate while swinging, garnered a second straight batting title. After hitting .381 in 1930, he bested himself with .390 in 1931.

The Redbirds spent a second season under the tutelage of Charles "Gabby" Street. His biggest accomplishments as a player had been serving as Walter Johnson's battery mate and catching a ball dropped off the Washington Monument. Now, his team owned a batting title holder in Chick Hafey and a leading pitcher with "Wild" Bill Hallahan. Yet neither league-leading Cardinal gained the notoriety enjoyed by the new center fielder, John Leonard Roosevelt Martin.

During Martin's minor league days, a Roch-ester sportswriter branded the Oklahoma native "The Wild Hoss of the Osage" for his high school football success. Others knew him as "Pepper," yet he disliked the nickname. Headfirst slides and clubhouse pranks were trademarks of Martin's, famed for never wearing underwear. Although he had a "cup of coffee" with the 1928 Cardinals, he was destined for part-time play until 1931. Trying to sell himself politely to non-swearing general manager Branch Rickey, Martin is famed for exclaiming, "John Brown! If you can't play me, Mr. Rickey, trade me." For the executive whose cussing never exceeded "Judas Priest," the words were well chosen.

Martin secured the Redbirds' rebound and championship grab, going .500 (12-for-24) with a homer, 5 RBI, and 5 steals in the 7-game battle. After the season, his newfound fame translated into a guest appearance in a vaudeville tour at $1,500 per week. Supposedly, Martin quit the stage because he was missing the hunting season back in Oklahoma.

As he did following the 1914 Series, when his favored club fell in postseason play, Mack began a systematic flushing of high-paid veterans from his ranks. In 1932, the 94–60 team finished second, 13 games behind the Yankees. Baseball's Grand Old Man would never lead his team to another World Series.

Representatives from both league champion teams were honored with a new tradition. The Baseball Writers' Association of America voted on MVPs for the first time, selecting Lefty Grove and St. Louis infielder Frankie Frisch.

Frisch broke in with the 1919 Giants, feted as the "Fordham Flash" for his direct move from college to the majors. He pulled double duty for the 1934 Cardinals, managing them to a pennant while playing in his eighth World Series.

How tough were the times? President Hoover came to the 1931 Series in Philadelphia to throw out the expected first ball. The crowd booed him, chanting, "We want beer!" With the onslaught of prohibition and the Depression, even presidents wouldn't get a third strike.

Brooklyn chose a new future in 1932, abandoning its "Robins" label. As Brooklyn became an urban hub at the turn of the century, residents

LEFT: *Philadelphia Athletics outfielder Al "Bucketfoot" Simmons began the decade on a tear. He was the American League's reigning batting king in 1930 and 1931, posting averages of .381 and .390, respectively. After he "slumped" to .322 in 1922 (with a league-leading 216 hits), Simmons was sold with Jimmy Dykes and Mule Haas to the White Sox.*

ABOVE: *Cardinals left fielder Charles "Chick" Hafey reflects in a portrait from September 1930. The 1931 NL batting champion with a .349 mark, Hafey was sent in a cost-cutting move to Cincinnati in exchange for Harvey Hendrick, Benny Frey, and some cash on April 11, 1932.*

BELOW: *Johnny "Pepper" Martin was a barrel-chested Cardinal who divided his time between third base and the outfield. Also known as "The Wild Hoss of the Osage" for his gung-ho play, Martin earned three NL stolen base crowns in the 1930s.*

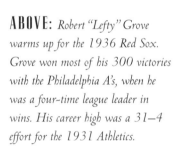

were nicknamed "Trolleydodgers." A shortened version became the team's new title.

Cleveland set an important off-field precedent with its radio broadcasts in 1932. Jack Graney was a local favorite, an ex-player who logged fourteen seasons with the Indians, dating back to 1908. When he moved to the broadcast booth, Graney became the first ex-player to announce, years before athletes were expected to become color commentators.

The Series would be a traditional 4-game Yankee sweep. Gehrig propelled the rout with 3 homers, 8 RBI, and a .529 average. Nevertheless, the headlines belonged to the Babe.

In what would be Ruth's final World Series appearance, he was 5-for-15 with 2 homers and 6 RBI. His Game Three performance created one of baseball's most enduring legends.

There was no love lost between the clubs. Yankees manager Joe McCarthy had been fired by the Cubs for finishing in second place in 1930. The Yankees despised their foes for another reason: long-time Yankees shortstop Mark Koenig had been swapped to Chicago in August, and despite his pennant-drive assistance (.353 in 33 games), the Cubs voted him just a half-share of Series profits before the event began.

Teams tossed charges back and forth, in newspapers and from benches. At Wrigley Field, fans

ABOVE: *Robert "Lefty" Grove warms up for the 1936 Red Sox. Grove won most of his 300 victories with the Philadelphia A's, when he was a four-time league leader in wins. His career high was a 31–4 effort for the 1931 Athletics.*

RIGHT: *Babe Ruth in pregame reflection before a home stand against the Red Sox on May 3, 1931. Though the pudgy home run machine had been injured and sidelined for the previous two weeks, he singled twice to help the Yankees to an 8–3 win.*

and Cubs heckled Ruth in the top of the fifth. With one out, myth was born. From the batter's box, Babe pointed. After a called strike, he pointed again, then slammed Charlie Root's letup over the center field wall.

Ruth alternated between confirming and denying that he "called" his shot. Cubs manager Charlie Grimm later explained that he thought Ruth pointed at bench-jockeying pitcher Guy Bush, goading him to take the mound. Regardless of the version, the episode has endured as sports lore.

Chicago experienced a second epic in baseball history in 1933. *Chicago Tribune* sports editor Arch Ward wanted a way for the majors to participate in the Chicago Exposition, a celebration of the city's centennial. His brainchild was an All-Star Game. Mack and McGraw (coming out of retirement) were selected to manage, based on their seniority.

The American League stars won the game, 4–3, on a 2-run homer by Ruth, the first in the event's history.

Although neither man would get World Series recognition, baseball sported two Triple Crown winners in 1933. Jimmie Foxx won his second

straight MVP for the A's, while Chuck Klein reached career highs for the Phillies. But baseball was still a business, and a funny one at that. Cash-strapped Philadelphia sold Klein to wealthy new Red Sox owner Tom Yawkey in the off-season.

Two familiar teams led by new generals made up the 1933 World Series. Washington had tried Senators great Walter Johnson as manager; however, owner Clark Griffith decided to keep the team a family affair. He installed twenty-six-year-old shortstop and son-in-law Joe Cronin as manager. Not only did Cronin supply solid leadership, but he chipped in with a .309 average and a team-leading 118 RBI.

For the Giants, John McGraw reluctantly relinquished managerial reins following 1932 because of high blood pressure and a poor prostate. His handpicked successor was "Memphis Bill" Terry. New York's 1933 championship was a farewell to McGraw. The team's leader for three decades didn't live to see another season, dying at the age of sixty on February 25, 1934.

In January 1934, Terry's joke to New York writers re-ignited one of baseball's oldest rivalries.

ABOVE, LEFT: *Cubs skipper Charlie Grimm (left) and Yankees manager Joe McCarthy (right) pose with New York Giants leader John McGraw before the second game of the 1932 World Series, when Vernon "Lefty" Gomez hurled the Yanks to a 6–2 win. McGraw's managerial career ended that year.*

ABOVE, RIGHT: *The Boston Red Sox needed Lyn Lary and $225,000 to obtain the services of shortstop Joe Cronin (pictured). A player-manager, Cronin supplied more punch than the average middle infielder. When he was with the Senators, he posted five consecutive years of 100-plus RBI.*

"Do you fear the Dodgers?" Rud Rennie of the New York *Herald-Tribune* inquired. "I was just wondering," answered the Giants manager, "whether they were still in the league."

By 1934, St. Louis was supplying the bulk of baseball's colorful characters. The team's in-the-dirt aggressiveness prompted one writer to remark that the players looked and acted like "the gang who works down at the gas house." Leading the oddball parade were two brothers, Jay and Paul Dean.

Fans preferred to label them "Dizzy" and "Daffy," respectively. Diz began a five-year blitz on the National League, winning 120 games and three strikeout championships. But writers appreciated covering his folksy wisdom even more than his pitching mastery. Dizzy, whose education went as far as the second grade, theorized: "If you can do it, it ain't braggin'." His prediction that he and Paul would win 45 games in 1934 was only slightly off. Paul won 19, and Dizzy added 30. The brothers would enjoy one more tandem bonanza in 1935, with 28 wins for Diz and 19 more for his overshadowed elder brother.

The 1934 Giants were but a minor challenge to the Cardinals. Yet in that year's All-Star Game, Giants hurler Carl Hubbell challenged everyone.

The lanky screwball artist crafted 5 straight strikeouts of the American League's finest—Ruth, Gehrig, Foxx, Simmons, and Cronin. From 1930 through 1939, he won 190 games.

RIGHT, TOP: *Bill Terry gave the New York Giants more than fine fielding as first baseman. The 1930 NL Most Valuable Player was chosen by John McGraw to become only the team's second manager in three decades. Terry won a pennant in his first year, adding first-place finishes in 1936 and 1937.*

RIGHT, BOTTOM: *Jimmie "Double X" Foxx flexes his long-ball muscles for the Philadelphia Athletics in 1932. Also known as "The Beast," Foxx threatened Babe Ruth's season-homer mark with 58 round-trippers. Frank "Home Run" Baker, then a minor league manager, discovered Foxx and sold him to the A's prior to the 1925 campaign.*

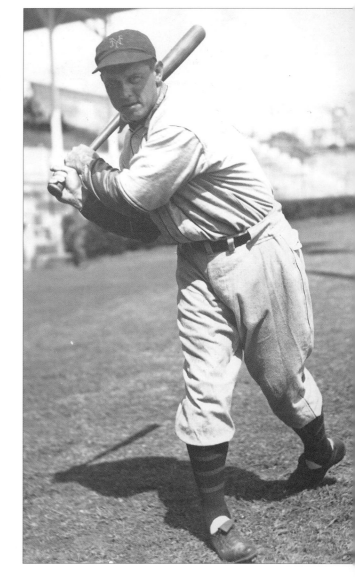

An era began to fade in 1935. Babe Ruth abandoned Yankees pinstripes to return to the town where he first tasted greatness. The Boston Braves gave Ruth the ceremonial and meaningless post of assistant manager to keep him playing part-time while drawing fans. The fading great retired in June, but not before hitting 3 homers in a game at Pittsburgh, including the first ever smacked completely out of Forbes Field. After only 28 games, Ruth was leaving the game with 6 homers, a dozen RBI, and a .181 average. His desire to become the Yankees' manager, which he constantly voiced to the press, fell on deaf ears. Babe could attract no more than a one-year stint coaching for Brooklyn in 1938.

The last non-Yankees World Series title of the thirties belonged to the 1935 Tigers. Catcher-manager Cochrane (one of the Philadelphia sell-offs) rallied his troops to a 6-game conquest after Hank Greenberg, who swatted 36 homers and 170 RBI during the regular season, was lost with a broken wrist after

Game Two. Cochrane would lead Detroit to second-place outcomes in 1936 and 1937 until a beaning by Yankee "Bump" Hadley fractured the skull of Black Mike in three places.

The life-threatening injury halted Cochrane's playing career, and in August 1938, new owner Walter Briggs unceremoniously fired him.

Because of Cincinnati's struggles in the thirties, the team became one of baseball's most important trendsetters of the decade. On May 24, 1935, the team installed permanent lighting, to give the majors their first night game. President Franklin D. Roosevelt was touted as turning on the first lights, by use of a remote control in Washington, D.C. Cubs owner William Wrigley allowed all his club's games to be featured on radio, a move once believed to kill ticket sales, just as clubs were facing potentially fatal

ABOVE: *Anointed by the press as "Daffy" and "Dizzy," brothers Paul (left) and Jay Dean each claimed 2 victories apiece against the Detroit Tigers in the 1934 World Series. Diz predicted that his family would combine for 45 wins. With 19 wins from Paul, the brothers collected 49 triumphs. One victory by Paul was a September no-hitter against the Brooklyn Dodgers.*

LEFT: *Discovered in the Tigers minor league system, Carl Hubbell became baseball's screwball master of the 1930s. The lefty won Most Valuable Player Awards in 1933 and 1936, amid his five-year run of 20-win seasons. Hubbell's left elbow became permanently crooked from years of screwballing.*

revenues. Even Pittsburgh acted to save its club. Pennsylvania blue laws were lifted, enabling the Pirates to host a Sunday game.

But attendance was at its shakiest in 1935. Strong, fast measures were needed. The St. Louis Browns drew only 80,922 spectators that year. For the entire decade, the Brownies would trail last in baseball crowds, with 1,184,076. Between 1930 and 1933, attendance had dropped by four million.

A major baseball boost premiered in 1936. Joseph Paul DiMaggio, the son of a San Francisco fisherman, started as a shortstop that year in the Pacific Coast League at age seventeen. His minor league credentials included a 61-game hitting streak in 1933. When the Yankees installed him in left field, he responded with 29 homers, 125 RBI, a .323 batting average, and a league-leading 22 assists. Such solid numbers were in spite of DiMaggio missing the first 16 games of the season because of a malfunctioning trainer's room machine that burned his foot during spring training.

DiMaggio roomed with Vernon "Lefty" Gomez and was befriended by other Bay Area natives on the team, including Tony Lazzeri and Frankie Crosetti. Gomez speculated on DiMaggio's immediate hero status, saying, "All the Italians in America adopted him. Everyone wanted to be Italian if they could get DiMaggio to come to their dinner."

Meanwhile, Cleveland unveiled pitching phenom Bob Feller in 1936, one full year before he was set to graduate from his Van Meter, Iowa, high school. By the end of that year, "Rapid Robert" was no secret. His high school graduation was covered nationally by NBC radio.

The 1937 All-Star Game marked the beginning of the end for Dizzy Dean. Cleveland's Earl Averill lined a shot off Dean's big toe. Even amid such drama, the press had a heyday. Supposedly, the doctor who examined Dean remarked, "This toe is fractured." Dean replied, "Fractured, hell! The damn thing's broken."

The laughs ended when Dean tried to come back too soon from the injury. He altered his pitching motion, which ultimately ruined his arm. On April 16, 1938, the Cardinals shuttled Dizzy to the Cubs for Curt Davis, Clyde Shoun, Tuck Stainback, and $185,000. Although Dean wasn't the dazzler

LEFT: *Joe DiMaggio cracks a single against the Senators in Washington, D.C., on April 30, 1938. The delayed season debut by DiMaggio was due to his contract holdout. "Joltin' Joe" warmed up quickly, however, ending with totals of 32 homers, 129 RBI, and a .324 batting average.*

BELOW, LEFT: *The first ball of the 1940 season was thrown by president Franklin D. Roosevelt and witnessed by postmaster James Farley (left), Senators owner Clark Griffith (second from left), Red Sox manager Joe Cronin (second from right), and Washington skipper Bucky Harris (right). "The president was obviously off his form, for the toss was so weak it didn't reach the ball players," remarked a sympathetic sportswriter. "A policeman standing in front of the grandstand caught it."*

BELOW, RIGHT: *At age seventeen, Joe DiMaggio (right) joined the San Francisco Seals of the Pacific Coast League. The outfielder left public school after the eleventh grade to pursue pro ball. Here, he poses with team manager Ike Caveney. Among his minor league feats was a 61-game hitting streak during the 1933 PCL season, a sign of things to come.*

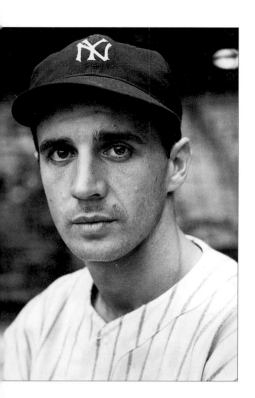

ABOVE: *Shortstop Frankie Crosetti started for the Yankees for three years before flexing any offensive muscle. His 1936 stats included 15 homers and 137 runs scored. Two years later, he paced the American League with 27 stolen bases.*

RIGHT: *Yankee Vernon "Lefty" Gomez became the American League's equivalent of Dizzy Dean, at least in the colorful quote derby. Sportswriters adored Gomez's quirky personality, praising him with a variety of nicknames: "Goofy," "The Gay Castillion," and "El Goofo." Gomez did his share of clutch pitching for the Yankees, however. While going 26–5 in 1934, he topped the American League in six categories.*

of the past, his 7–1 record and 1.81 ERA helped Chicago win that year's pennant.

The Cincinnati Reds rose from the ashes of last place in 1937 to 1939's pennant. Yet they were literal washouts in the National League. Mammoth flooding from the Ohio River that year poured over the center and left field walls, swamping the park, which sat nearly ten feet below street level. But just one year later, the Reds would see one of their least likely prospects earn a bit of immortality.

Left-hander Johnny Vander Meer spent the bulk of his 1937 rookie campaign with the Reds in relief. His 3–5 record and 3.84 ERA in 19 games neared no records. Then the hurler, whose lineage earned him "The Dutch Master" as a nickname, spun 2 consecutive no-hit games in the middle of Cincy's pennant drive.

Vander Meer's second no-hit masterpiece happened within a larger backdrop. On June 15, 1938, Ebbets Field was hosting its first-ever night game.

Manager "Deacon" Bill McKechnie, architect of the Cincy overhaul, had won pennants with two previous clubs, the 1925 Pirates and the 1928 Cardinals. "I can sincerely say that I was proud to play

OPPOSITE: *Iowa farmboy Bob Feller became a fastballing legend in Cleveland, getting his first pro experience as a teenager. Dubbed "Rapid Robert" and the "Heater from Van Meter" (his hometown), Feller's high school graduation became a national news event covered by radio and newspapers.*

ABOVE: *After consecutive 15-win seasons for the White Sox in 1937 and 1938, pitcher Monte Stratton's career was snuffed out at age twenty-six. While rabbit hunting, Stratton accidentally shot his right knee with a pistol, requiring a subsequent leg amputation.*

RIGHT: *Cincinnati's Johnny Vander Meer, shown here during 1937 spring training, was one year away from making baseball history during his 1938 sophomore season. His second consecutive no-hitter spoiled Brooklyn's first-ever night game at Ebbets Field. A fourth-inning single yielded to the Boston Braves in a subsequent start produced an NL record of 21 straight hitless innings.*

for him," Vander Meer said. "He was one of the greatest individuals I ever met in my life, either on the field or off. Ballplayers never feared McKechnie; they respected him."

In the American League, Detroit's Hank Greenberg became another threat to Ruth's single-season home run marks. The Tigers outfielder's power was no secret. In 1937, he drove in a league-record 183 runs, only to lose the MVP award to teammate Charley Gehringer and his league-best .371 average. A year later, Greenberg carved out 56 homers in his first 148 games. In the next game, he hit a pair out, and seemed guaranteed of setting a new record. But public pressure to make history drove Greenberg into a season-ending slump. In fact, Greenberg's last game was a 4-for-8 performance with none leaving the park. His failure to top Ruth was masked by nineteen-year-old Feller's 18 strikeouts. A record was set, after all.

Before the 1939 season began, news of a tragedy spread. Monte Stratton's future with the White Sox rotation had looked bright, but that was before an off-season hunting accident left the young pitcher with one leg.

The Yankees defended their pennant in 1939, as their 106 wins led the league by a 17-game margin. Their season was far from unblemished, though. The year started with team owner Colonel Jacob Ruppert dying from phlebitis at age seventy-one. The biggest shock was seeing Lou Gehrig take himself out of the lineup on May 2. Babe Dahlgren would shoulder the task of replacing "Larrupin' Lou."

On June 21, the world was told that Gehrig suffered from a rare form of polio. Decades would pass before the illness would finally be understood as amyotrophic lateral sclerosis, often called Lou Gehrig's disease.

That Fourth of July at Yankee Stadium attracted sixty-two thousand fans for a ceremonial tribute. Wiping away tears, Gehrig said goodbye. "I consider myself the luckiest man on the face of the earth," said the man who Joe McCarthy feared wouldn't be able to stand without assistance.

The crosstown Dodgers weren't silent in 1939. Shortstop Leo "The Lip" Durocher was named player-manager. On August 26, Brooklyn hosted Cincinnati and the future. NBC television, through station W2XBS, broadcast the medium's first major league baseball game. That May, NBC had warmed up with a collegiate broadcast of Columbia versus Princeton. However, that telecast didn't benefit from two-camera technology, or from the southern eloquence of broadcaster Red Barber.

Just as New York had obtained DiMaggio, Boston imported a slugger from the Pacific Coast League, named Theodore Samuel Williams.

Washington, D.C.'s Griffith Stadium was the site of this historic pose prior to the 1937 All-Star Game. Lou Gehrig, Joe Cronin, Bill Dickey, Joe DiMaggio, Charlie Gehringer, Jimmie Foxx, and Hank Greenberg (from left to right) were all smiles before the contest. Although Gehrig's 4 RBI created an 8—3 win, the game wasn't without drama. Cleveland's Earl Averill lined a pitch off Dizzy Dean, resulting in a broken toe.

LEFT, TOP: *The decade ended with sadness, as ailing star Lou Gehrig said goodbye. In a July 4 tribute at Yankee Stadium, Gehrig uttered the immortal echo of gratitude: "Today, I consider myself the luckiest man on the face of the earth." He served in a ceremonial assistant's post to the mayor of New York in the months just before his death.*

LEFT, BELOW: *Detroit's powerful trio of "G Men" in the 1930s were (from left to right) Leon "Goose" Goslin, Hank Greenberg, and Charlie Gehringer. The Tigers became 1935 world champions on the backs of the three eventual Hall of Famers, leading the American League in team batting average, slugging percentage, and runs scored.*

Young shortstop Leo Durocher (left) and Babe Ruth pose for this 1929 snapshot. The infielder would spend the thirties in the National League, however. First finding fame as a scrappy part of the 1934 "Gas House Gang" world champions in St. Louis, Durocher went on to join the 1939 Dodgers as player-manager. His first-year leadership produced a third-place 84–69 result.

Although the world championship continued to rest in New York City, baseball earned a symbolic home upstate that year, in the village of Cooperstown. In 1936, Ford Frick, then NL president, conceived the idea of Cooperstown as a permanent locale for a museum and Hall of Fame. The idea became reality in 1939, the centennial of Abner Doubleday's "invention." Voted upon by the 226-member Baseball Writers' Association of America from an AL-prepared list in 1936, the first players selected to the Hall of Fame were Ty Cobb (222 votes), Honus Wagner (215), Babe Ruth (215), Christy Mathewson (205), and Walter Johnson (189). A total of twenty-six inductions would be made before the Hall opened. The biggest drama of the day was Cobb's late arrival at

the ceremonies, missing the first group picture. Later, he confessed to skipping the picture to avoid commissioner Landis, whom he still hated for his not offering more support during the 1926 gambling accusations.

On June 12, a ceremony unveiled "the church of baseball," a place where fans could flock to rediscover baseball's history and mystery. A total of eleven inductees were on hand, along with the spirits of posthumous members Mathewson and Wee Willie Keeler.

No matter how contrived the "birthplace of baseball" idea may have been, baseball now had a resting place for its history. The museum came just in time, for the coming decade would be filled with one of baseball's most historic casts.

CHAPTER SIX
1940–1949

"**D**on't you know there's a war on?"

The 1940s began with such cries of patriotism from citizens struggling with food rationing, travel restrictions, and unpredictably uneven baseball.

Baseball would soon face hardships. Rosters would be gutted for the first part of the decade as players were drafted into the armed forces. Teams were forced to scrape up retirees, teenagers, or any other able-bodied 4-F who could pass for a player.

Not in 1940, though. The Reds retained the nucleus of their 1939 pennant winner, which resulted in 20-game winners Bucky Walters and Paul Derringer. AL champion Detroit still cruised on Greenberg's power, which produced 41 homers and 150 RBI. First baseman Rudy York was a converted catcher, adding 33 dingers and 140 RBI. The Tigers won their league by 1 game, edging out Cleveland and AL-pacing Bob Feller's 27 wins.

One Red turned a tragedy into one of the greatest World Series comeback tales. In August, catcher Ernie Lombardi was injured. Reserve catcher Willard Hershberger, had gone out to dinner with manager Bill McKechnie to discuss his mediocre play. Hershberger confessed that he had contemplated suicide. The next day, he failed to show up for a doubleheader against the Braves. He was found dead in his hotel room, his throat cut with a razor.

The team turned to forty-year-old coach Jimmie Wilson, an ex-receiver who batted just five times in 1938–1939. He hit .353 in postseason play, recorded the only stolen base of the 7 games, and caught 2 complete-game wins each from Walters and Derringer. Wilson's extra contribution brought more than a World Series winners' share. He received the manager's job from the 1941 Cubs.

The American League featured two milestones in 1941. The first began on May 15, when Joe DiMaggio singled against the White Sox. Through the month of June, "The Yankee Clipper" kept hitting, game after game. The second involved the Yankees great who didn't live to see the streaking DiMaggio. Lou Gehrig died at his home on June 2. On June 19, he would have turned thirty-eight.

OPPOSITE: *Ted Williams (left) and Joe DiMaggio must have been imagining their home run potentials in certain NL bandboxes during this photo, taken July 12, 1949, before the All-Star Game at cozy Ebbets Field. Even without such a long-ball advantage, Williams would win four AL home run titles in the 1940s, ending with a career-high 43 in 1949. DiMaggio was fresh from leading the junior circuit with 39 home runs in 1948.*

MEET HISTORY'S INVISIBLE COACH

The idea of a team "coach" dates back to 1908, when Cleveland's "Deacon" Jim McGuire and the Phillies' William "Kid" Gleason became the first paid nonplaying assistants to the managers. Although Gleason had been Philadelphia's team captain from 1905 to 1907, both had been hired primarily as backup players. Their leadership and guidance out of the lineup proved to be added bonuses. Both teams initially sought them because they were successful veteran players.

Other historians have assigned the glory of hiring the first coach to John McGraw and the 1909 Giants, who employed Arlie Latham exclusively as a baseline coach. Latham's role was just as quizzical as Gleason and McGuire's. Latham, who had played in the 1880s, gained later fame primarily as an on-field cheerleader who heckled foes and clowned for fans.

Even through the teens, clubs were slow to hire a full-time coach. Pitchers had served as coaches between starts, saving teams extra salaries. A veteran, or the manager, would serve as a base coach. Actually, baseball's early rules stopped teams from placing more than one coach on the field at once, forcing the coach to alternate between first and third base.

When clubs did hire coaches, nearly all had spent time as major league players. And there was usually only one coach, who would serve as an assistant manager. In fact, in the Phillies media guide, the team doesn't even credit Gleason as a coach. The first coach noted, Jesse Tannehill, was a member of the 1920 (last-place) team managed by Gavvy Cravath. Before that, Tannehill was a pitcher-outfielder for seven teams from 1894 through 1911.

Baseball's first coaches never landed official titles like "batting coach." Few ever made it onto a baseball card. Many are ignored in the all-time rosters updated by teams. At the most, a club will offer a one-line listing of a coach's name and his years of service.

Albert Linder Vincent was only the fourth man in history to become a coach in the majors without a game's worth of big-league playing experience. As an eighty-eight-year-old Texas retiree, he wrote this description of his career.

My coaching years were as follows:
Detroit, 1943–44
Baltimore, 1955–59
Philadelphia Phillies, 1961–63
Kansas City, 1966–67

In those years, we all primarily "worked." Fungo hitting, batting-practice pitching, special assignment, and voluntary coaching anywhere it was needed that you were qualified to render aid, all at the approval of the manager. Having been a teaching manager in the Detroit organization for many years, I felt and feel there is no department in which I could not coach effectively.

Coaches are nonentities by and large, and lose their identity in the job, the exception being an established star giving a coach credit. It happens, but all too seldom.

I started as a player in the lower minors in 1928; I was born December 23, 1906. I started managing in the Texas League in 1937. Then after four years, I went to Buffalo in the International League for two years, 1941–42. Then to Detroit in 1943–44. Scouted a year, and in 1946, took the job as manager at Dallas, when the Texas League started backup (having been closed during part of World War II) and was there 1946–47. Then to Tulsa, 1948–51. Then to Baltimore in 1955.

I can name many players who went from my clubs to the major leagues. You would have to ask them if they were aided by my efforts.

To name a few: Dizzy Trout, Virgil Trucks, Barney McCosky, Pat Mullin, Les Fleming, Frank Secory, Botts Poffenberger, Hal Newhouser, Fred Hutchinson, Frank Smith, Walter Perkowski, Wally Post, Joe Adcock, Johnny Temple, Roy McMillan, Alex Grammas, Joe Nuxhall. There were a few who became managers, such as Hutchinson, Danny Ozark, Mayo Smith, Jack Tighe, Adcock, and a couple more I can't recall.

Coaches are more specified today. Apparently, some things are theirs to handle. So they have more responsibility, I assume. And I am sure they sink or swim, dependent upon their productiveness.

Ballplayers (as in anything) do not learn and/or correct things in a day—nor are they expected to. It can happen, but more than likely, it will take time to assimilate changes.

Check the record to see what the major league clubs did in the few years "after" I had left them.

A few facts: I was the first to bring grass up to the baseline on the first- and third-base lines. A bunt rolling off the grass is foul—eliminates cheating on sloping the dirt to suit your own club. Less dirt to be muddy—a help to groundskeeping.

I was the first to talk the Texas League into using carbon-copy lineups at home plate, eliminating mistakes on three separately made cards.

In 1938, used football helmets for 5 innings at bat, the first, as far as I know.

I suggested making the big catcher's mitt so Hoyt Wilhelm could use his knuckler without so much fear of passed balls with men on base—especially third. This suggestion was quickly adopted by the Baltimore club.

From 1946 to 1950, my clubs at Dallas and Tulsa played 77 postseason games.

I should have been qualified to coach!

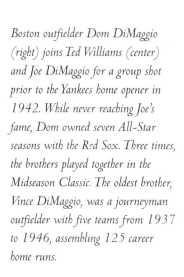

Boston outfielder Dom DiMaggio (right) joins Ted Williams (center) and Joe DiMaggio for a group shot prior to the Yankees home opener in 1942. While never reaching Joe's fame, Dom owned seven All-Star seasons with the Red Sox. Three times, the brothers played together in the Midseason Classic. The oldest brother, Vince DiMaggio, was a journeyman outfielder with five teams from 1937 to 1946, assembling 125 career home runs.

Even in the All-Star Game, DiMaggio doubled. His streak survived until July 17, when little-known Cleveland hurlers Al Smith and Jim Bagby, Jr., were feted not only for holding DiMag hitless, but for limiting him to infield grounders.

Who could top such a record? Boston's Ted Williams, already facing countless comparisons to the Yankees outfielder, was pursuing his own path to excellence. In the All-Star Game, his bottom-of-the-ninth 3-run homer gave the American League a come-from-behind 7–5 win.

Williams could have protected his .400 mark (.39955) the last day of the season, if he had skipped the final doubleheader in Philadelphia. Instead, he chose to play. To quote Williams, "To hell with that. I don't want anybody saying I got in through the back door." Responding with efforts of 4-for-5 and 6-for-8, Williams finished the season with a .406 average.

Brooklyn dethroned the Reds as NL champions while sporting baseball's nearly modern version of the batting helmet. The Dodgers fell fast, how-

ever, in 5 Series games. Of the Yankees romp, New York's Game Four win stands out. With two out in the ninth and the Dodgers ahead, Yankee Tommy Henrich appeared to strike out. But the third strike squirted away from catcher Mickey Owen, opening the door for a 7–4 comeback.

Although writers tagged Owen as the Series "goat," the receiver carried a 1941 NL record into the next year. Before his streak ended in 1942, Owen had handled 509 straight chances without an error. An interesting oddity of the Series is that Henrich, nicknamed "Old Reliable," struck out just 40 times during the regular season.

One year after Gehrig died, Gary Cooper depicted the Hall of Famer in the critically acclaimed movie *Pride of the Yankees*. In a small but convincing part, Babe Ruth played himself.

The Yankees would lose the 1942 Series in 5 games. St. Louis disbanded its "Gas House Gang," but included a rookie outfielder named Stanley Frank Musial. Growing up in Donora, Pennsylvania, Musial played on high school teams with Ken

GROWING UP TOGETHER IN NEW ENGLAND
As Told by Ray Medeiros

I learned about Ted Williams in 1941. I was seven years old, just a peanut. I had scraped together a couple of pennies and bought a couple of packs of Play Ball cards (which were only a penny per pack then).

I was sitting at the table, having lunch with my mom and dad. I pulled out a card of Soupy Campbell [Clarence Campbell, a reserve outfielder with the Indians], which floored me. I said, with a name like "Soupy," this guy must be good.

"No, Ray," said my Dad, thumbing through my cards. "This is the guy." He showed me a card of Ted Williams. Until then, I didn't know who the heck he was, this guy who was playing ball only 50 miles north of Fall River [Massachusetts], where I lived. I learned.

For the next four years, I was more interested in comic books than baseball. The only part of the newspaper I wanted was the comics page. In 1945, I began listening to Red Sox games on the radio and reading the sports pages. The first game I ever attended was on September 9, 1945, the Tigers at Fenway, but the only star in either lineup was Hank Greenberg.

It was late May in 1946 when I first saw Williams play, a Sunday doubleheader. It was a great treat for everyone. All the regulars—Williams, Dom DiMaggio, Bobby Doerr, and Johnny Pesky—were back from World War II. Joe DiMaggio, Phil Rizzuto, and Bill Dickey came back for the Yankees. While the Sox split the pair, Williams had only one single for both games.

In 1947, I saw Williams really produce for the first time. Versus the White Sox, he homered into the right-field bullpen, a towering drive that seemed to soar into the clouds. I remember that Williams and Joe DiMaggio would get ovations after they took batting practice. It was pretty special for the spectators.

Where I grew up, with the exception of a couple of kids who were Yankee fans, Williams was idolized. He was known as "the Thumper" in my neighborhood. That was my favorite nickname. I don't remember anyone ever getting down on Williams, even after he hit .200 in the 1946 World Series. I think that in Massachusetts, many of his detractors were generally older fans who retained an allegiance to Babe Ruth and Tris Speaker from the 1912–18 period.

I had a lot of mixed feelings when teams pulled defensive shifts against him. It seemed like dirty pool, but he didn't show he was a smart hitter initially. I felt he should be able to go the other way. Here was my idol, failing because of vanity and stupidity. Within a year, he made the adjustments.

I didn't read the Boston papers each day. I think writers for papers outside of Boston may have been more respectful to Williams and all the Red Sox. But papers like the Post and the Daily Record antagonized fans. For circulation wars, it was a great way to sell papers. Williams was an easy target for big screaming headlines.

I'd always get to Fenway two hours before game time, to watch teams take warm-ups and batting practice. Back then, ushers would let kids get all the way down to the front row of box seats. Williams had a habit of standing behind the batting cage. I remember hearing him talk, yelling out to opposing players. We kids would be only about 25 feet away. He never worried about fraternizing.

The kids I knew weren't aware of seeing players out of uniform, on the street. If we read about the Red Sox stars like Williams attending a public banquet, it was usually in the city. Kids like myself didn't think it was possible to meet a player. Kids in Maine had a better shot at meeting him, because he'd go there to fish.

I never hung around for autographs. After the last pitch, I rushed for the exit from the ballpark in search of the newspaper boys hawking copies of the latest editions. At that time, papers were published in numerous editions each day. You'd find a copy with a story and

Some Boston sportswriters gave the impression that Ted Williams never smiled. "Teddy Ballgame" endured an ongoing rhubarb with some of the media in the 1950s. Once, he was assessed a $5,000 fine by the owner of the Red Sox for spitting defiantly in the direction of the press box in the middle of a home run trot. He mockingly called his newspaper foes "knights of the keyboard."

results covering the game you just saw, through the seventh inning.

I only remember lingering outside Fenway once after a game. I saw Williams in a 1951 Cadillac. I had never seen power windows work on a car before. I was more amazed by that than by seeing my idol drive right past me.

Williams was businesslike at bat. During pregame drills in the field, he was animated with teammates, but not with any fans. He always acted unaware that anyone was watching from the stands. Yet on the field with others, he didn't seem as aloof as I thought Joe DiMaggio was. I definitely felt DiMaggio was a loner. Williams loved tossing the ball around before games. He'd act as if he were a pitcher (which he was in the minors). He'd be having a good time, throwing curves and sinkers.

In the spring of 1947, I cut out the picture from The Sporting News showing Williams talking to Paul Waner in spring training. The caption said they were discussing the art of hitting to the opposite field. Williams says now that he never tried intentionally to hit to left. I don't believe it. I remember seeing him shift his feet often!

I remember playing ball with kids in a cramped school yard. We'd all bat left-handed, so we'd be hitting away from the windows. We'd all imitate Williams, even down to shifting our feet at bat.

Williams was all business in the field, too. Some writers hung on the fact that he was sloppy and inattentive with the glove in 1939. His fielding improved every year after that, though. I'd watch the pregame fielding drills, which included outfielders at Fenway, something teams don't do anymore. I was an outfielder and I wanted to learn how to throw like my heroes. Even before games, Williams' throws to home plate would come in like line drives.

I have a scrapbook, a foot and a half thick, devoted to Williams. It dates back to when he played high school baseball. My feelings about him haven't changed much. I've acquired an even greater admiration for him. I've seen him as a civilian, signing autographs at card shows, and I've talked with members of the air force who knew Williams [as a pilot] during

The familiar background framing Williams is that of the Red Sox spring training camp, then in Sarasota, Florida. After his retirement, the avid fisherman became a full-time Florida resident.

the Korean War. They all said he was professional and did his job without complaining. That makes me feel good.

○ ○ ○ ○ ○

Madieros is a baseball historian who lives in Colorado Springs, California.

Griffey, Jr.'s grandfather. The two teams would reverse roles the following year.

Enter Bill Veeck, Jr. His father had been president of the Chicago Cubs from 1919 until 1933, when the fifty-five-year-old executive died from influenza. His son left college to become a Cubs office boy.

Veeck learned the entire team's inner workings. He helped build Wrigley Field's gigantic manual scoreboard in 1937, and he planted 200 Boston ivy and 350 Japanese bittersweet plants to give the outfield walls their distinctive trademark.

Philip K. Wrigley ran the Cubs after the death of his father, William, in 1932. "P.K." had purchased lights for Wrigley Field, which waited inside the park to be installed. However, he ended up contributing the fixtures to the military in America's World War II effort on December 8, 1941, one day after the Japanese bombed Pearl Harbor.

Wrigley founded the All-American Girls Professional Baseball League in 1943, setting up franchises in Racine and Kenosha, Wisconsin; South Bend, Indiana; and Rockford, Illinois. The

TOP, LEFT: *Tommy "Old Reliable" Henrich was a right field fixture for the Yankees in the forties. Shown here in 1946, Henrich began his pro career buried in the Indians farm system, but was freed contractually by Commissioner Landis. The five-time All-Star would lead the American League in triples twice.*

TOP, RIGHT: *Stan Musial displays his cobralike batting pose before a game on June 21, 1948. A freak shoulder injury in his youth forced the Pennsylvania native to end his brief pitching career, which was unfortunate for the NL hurlers he went on to terrorize with his offense.*

LEFT: *Chicago Cubs owner P.K. Wrigley fretted over baseball's survival during World War II. He created the All-American Girls Professional Baseball League to sustain fan interest until major league males returned from military duty. Even after the war ended, though, the AAGPBL thrived for nearly a decade.*

A BROWNIES BRIGADE MEMBER REMEMBERS

As Told by Frank "Bud" Kane

I saw my first Browns game in 1936. I grew up as part of a big, extended family. My dad and uncles were Brownies fans, which dated back to the 1920s when the team was winning. Older people tended to be Browns fans, while kids who grew up with the Gashouse Gang liked the Cardinals. Either way, it was a loyalty you grew up with. But it wasn't like Chicago. Everyone in St. Louis supported both teams.

Compared to the Cardinals, the Brownies were dull. Because there weren't as many fans at Browns games, you could move around the ballpark [changing seats]. I remember going to my first game. Even on Grand Avenue, I kept asking, "Where's the ballpark?" I was looking for a park like the vacant lot we played ball on. But as a six-year-old, I was completely entranced by the sight of the field at Sportsman's Park. Once I saw the big left-field scoreboard, I was hooked for life.

The scoreboard, all operated by hand, was part of the fun of being there. You'd get an inning-by-inning line score of every game in both leagues posted. You'd even see when a team had changed pitchers.

I was there for the first night game in St. Louis history on May 24, 1940. Cleveland's Bob Feller pitched against our Eldon Auker. Almost 25,000 people attended, which seemed like a great crowd for a Browns game. The Indians won 3–2 on a homer hit by Feller. I met Feller almost fifty years later and asked him about the game. "Sure, I remember. I hit my first home run that night," he said with a huge grin. In the beginning, only 7 night games a year were allowed.

Some schools in St. Louis let classes off on opening day afternoon, but not Saint Luke's, where I went. My friend George Gaffney and I had agreed at recess that we had to get to the game. The problem was to come up with a believable excuse for Sister Bernard to let us off for the afternoon so that she wouldn't call our mothers. I claimed that my aunt had died and I had to go to the wake, while George had to go to the dentist. We both received skeptical looks, and Sister Bernard made George open wide and show her the cavity, but we were free!

By pooling our financial resources, we each had enough for streetcar fare (10 cents), a scorecard (5 cents), a hot dog (15 cents), and a Coke (10 cents). Outlaw scorecards sold outside the ballpark were cheaper than the official version printed by the Browns. Of course, we got in free with our Browns Brigade cards [the Browns version of the Cardinals Knothole Gang program, which allowed kids free admission].

With the Browns versus the Cardinals in the 1944 World Series, it was known as the "Streetcar Series." I was lucky enough to see 3 of the games and didn't have to ride the streetcar. My father somehow got tickets and we took the good ol' '39 Ford to the ballpark instead of the usual streetcar. Our seats were in the lower grandstand, between home and first base, behind the visiting dugout. We saw Games One, Two, and Six, when the Cardinals were home team (even though all games were in Sportsman's Park).

The Cardinals were favored heavily. But the Series was so close, with 4 of the 6 games decided by 1 or 2 runs, that it could have gone either way. After the Browns won 2 of the first 3 games, my dad and uncles were needling me about how they could win it all.

In the early days, we had four St. Louis radio stations to choose from for games. I tended to listen to Dizzy Dean, who was hired as an announcer by the Falstaff Brewery in 1941. You never knew what Dizzy would say or do.

My favorite Brown was Harland Clift, a power hitter who was a low-key type of guy. Infielder Don Gutteridge was a pepperpot. John Berardino was known in St. Louis as "Hollywood John," even before he retired and starred in a TV soap opera.

I've been a member of the St. Louis Browns Fan Club since it was organized in 1984. It's fun reminiscing with other fans and former players. They have good memories of the team, ballpark, and city. We never have trouble getting Browns to come back to our banquet year after year. Some people coming to a first meeting call beforehand to ask if the players are willing to sign autographs.

I think the surviving Browns are happy someone still wants their autographs!

○ ○ ○ ○ ○

Kane is a retired Missouri state employee who lives in St. Louis.

A bevy of Browns caught Cardinal George "Whitey" Kurowski in a second-inning rundown play during the sixth game of the 1944 World Series. Although New York and Chicago had hosted crosstown Fall Classics before, this compact contest featured all the games at Sportsman's Park in St. Louis (the home ballpark for both teams).

AAGPBL women would make history in Wrigley Field on July 1, 1943. Using portable, temporary lighting systems, two All-Star teams played exhibitions to raise money for the Women's Army Air Corps. Two WAAC teams rounded out the twin bill, witnessed by seven thousand fans. Four teams returned for a doubleheader on July 18, 1944, with free admission for the military, uniformed Red Cross members, or anyone who donated blood. Women gave Wrigley Field its first night baseball more than four decades before the Cubs could.

Veeck was blocked by commissioner Landis when he tried to head a group purchasing the 1943 Phillies. Veeck's intentions to stock the team with black stars from the Negro Leagues was too objectionable. "I try not to break the rules, but merely to test their elasticity," Veeck once said. Throughout the forties and the following three decades, he would remain baseball's first and best promoter.

No one doubted that the Phillies needed help, both in the box office and on the field. The team was temporarily renamed the Blue Jays in 1944–1945, either to revive fan interest or to disguise the identities of the losers.

As the war continued, clubs continued to beat the bushes for players. The press focused on the number of major leaguers drafted or enlisted in the military. Meanwhile, the minor leagues faced a double dipping. Any players who weren't snatched by the armed services were netted for the majors. Even the balls needed help. Baseballs were being manufactured from reprocessed rubber, creating a "deadened" sphere that lessened offenses.

Baseball's thin ranks were typified by the 1944 Reds. A fifteen-year-old pitcher from Hamilton, Ohio, was relieving against the Cardinals less than two months after signing a contract. Joe Nuxhall closed the game with two-thirds of an inning pitched, only after the nervous youth surrendered 5 runs on 5 walks and 2 hits.

Before 1944, fans believed that the only crosstown World Series could be held in New York. That was before the war blessed the St. Louis Browns. With only 89 wins, they earned an AL pennant.

Surprisingly, the Brownies weren't as hapless as was believed. They owned 2 victories in the first 3 games. Although the Cardinals prevailed, the Browns were only outscored by a slim 16–12 edge in 6 games. Because the teams shared Sportsman's Park, the Series was held there on six consecutive days, October 4 to 9.

One of the most memorable Browns was outfielder Pete Gray. He lost his right forearm in a childhood accident with a truck, but could still bat with one arm. For fielding, he would rest his glove under his partial arm, pass the ball across his chest, then throw left-handed. His only big-league year was with the 1945 Browns, batting .218 in 77 games. In 61 games in the field, he made 7 errors while recording 162 putouts. Demoted in 1946 when prewar players returned, Gray kept playing with barnstorming clubs until the early fifties.

Everyone got a chance during wartime. Ex–minor leaguer Bert Shepard was a pilot who had been shot down over Germany during World War II. With an artificial leg, he returned to coach

ABOVE: *Jean Marlowe, a native of Scranton, Pennsylvania, loosens her pitching arm for the Chicago Colleens of the All-American Girls Professional Baseball League during 1948 spring training. Ironically, Chicago wouldn't field an AAGPBL team until after Cubs owner P.K. Wrigley sold off his controlling interest in the league.*

BELOW, LEFT: *The St. Louis Browns used Pete Gray as a part-time outfielder for 77 games in 1945. With baseball's ranks depleted due to military service, the team fielded many surprising substitutes to keep the games going. Using the one-armed player was far from a publicity stunt, however. Gray had a distinguished three-year career in the minors (including 1944 Southern Association MVP honors) before advancing to the bigs.*

OPPOSITE: *Jack Roosevelt Robinson broke in with the 1947 Dodgers as a first baseman. His accomplishments as a second baseman with the 1945 Kansas City Monarchs of the Negro American League led to his discovery by Brooklyn scout Clyde Sukeforth.*

for Washington in 1945. On August 14, Shepard pitched 5 innings of relief against the Red Sox, yielding only 1 run.

The last wartime World Series would feature the Cubs against the Tigers, teams that had last met a decade earlier. Detroit regained Greenberg after his early May discharge from the army. Pitcher Virgil Trucks returned from the navy in August. Those additions, combined with "Prince Hal" Newhouser, gave the Bengals the pennant over Washington by 1½ games.

Harold Newhouser was a twenty-four-year-old pitcher whose royal nickname was first given because of his fits of anger as a rookie. After he sported a career-best 29 wins in 1944, followed by back-to-back MVP awards in 1944 and 1945, he was known as the king of remaining pitchers. A heart murmur kept him out of military service. Today, he's unfairly tagged as being a winner only in wartime. Newhouser won 26 against "real" players in 1946, and ended the decade as baseball's ten-year leader in wins (170) and strikeouts (1,578).

The biggest baseball news of the 1945 season was announced on October 23. The Montreal Royals had signed Jack Roosevelt Robinson to a minor league contract.

Branch Rickey had signed a five-year contract as Brooklyn's general manager in 1942, less than a month after the Cardinals' world championship. He hoped to help integrate baseball, a motive contributing to his move: Rickey noted that "St. Louis never permitted Negro patrons in the grandstand." After Veeck was rebuffed in his efforts to add Negro Leaguers to the Phillies, Rickey moved slowly and secretly. He met with Robinson on August 28, 1945, but insisted that no public comment be made. To try to gain some leverage, Rickey had previously hinted that he wanted to form his own Negro league.

By 1946, the Cardinals regained their prewar ranks. They tied the Dodgers at season's end for the pennant, with both teams at 96–58. For the first time, a playoff was needed to determine a World Series participant.

St. Louis grabbed 2 straight in the best-of-three duel. Two clutch strikeouts by Harry Brecheen earned a save and previewed his plans for the World Series against the Red Sox. Instead of becoming a duel between 1946 MVPs

Stan Musial and Ted Williams, the Redbirds won in 7 games behind "Country" and "The Cat."

Nicknamed for his felinelike quickness, Brecheen hurled a collection of screwballs at Boston, coming away with 3 wins, including 2 complete-game triumphs after a pair of starts. Previously, no lefty had ever had 3 Series triumphs. Enos "Country" Slaughter, who led the Cardinals with 18 homers and 130 RBI during the regular season, scored the winning run in Game Seven. A Harry Walker double seemed shallow enough to send Slaughter only to third. That was before he ignored the stop sign of third-base coach Mike Gonzales and made his "Mad Dash."

Slaughter remembered the event:

Well, I don't see nothin' unusual about that play. I think I just caught the whole Red Sox infield nappin' is all. If Bobby Doerr or Pinky Higgins would've hollered, "Home with it!" to [shortstop Johnny] Pesky—because he had his back to the infield, remember, when he took the throw from Leon Culberson—they probably would've thrown me out by 10 feet.

Brooklyn began the 1947 campaign in the public eye, even after seeing a pennant evaporate. As commissioner Landis was replaced by Happy Chandeler, Rickey saw his opportunity. Jackie Robinson was promoted from his year in the minors and handed the opening-day first baseman's job. He'd go on to win Rookie of the Year (back when baseball gave one award for both leagues), while leading the National League with 29 stolen bases.

Shortstop Harold "Pee Wee" Reese was the first teammate to support Robinson's arrival openly. In spring training, some southern-born Dodgers started a petition to avoid playing baseball with blacks. The Kentucky-born Reese had grown up where segregation was in effect, but refused to participate. During a home series that April, Phillies manager Ben Chapman derided all the Dodgers with racial taunts. During pregame infield practice, he mockingly yelled at Reese, asking how he liked playing with a "nigra." Without a word, Reese trotted over to first, threw his arm around Robinson's shoulders, and faced Chapman.

LEFT: *Hometown hurler Harold "Prince Hal" Newhouser was rejected from military service due to a heart defect. The Detroit native displayed lots of heart for his Tigers, peaking with a 25–9 mark and 1.81 ERA for the 1945 squad.*

ABOVE: *Enos "Country" Slaughter's "Mad Dash," which scored the winning run in the 1946 World Series, wasn't enough to guarantee a lifetime job in St. Louis. Although he broke in with the Cardinals in 1938, Slaughter was dealt to the Yankees in 1954. "I can't even talk. This is the most awful thing that has ever happened to me in my life," he said upon hearing of his departure.*

RIGHT: *Harold "Pee Wee" Reese wasn't tiny at five feet ten inches. In fact, the Brooklyn shortstop and Kentucky native loomed large amid the arrival of Jackie Robinson. Reese's on-field friendship with Robinson helped lessen the tension of integration.*

Years later, Reese still avoided speeches. "People tell me that I helped Jackie," he once said. "But knowing my background and the progress I've made, I have to say he helped me as much as I helped him."

The Dodgers didn't change the attitude of baseball owners overnight. Integration came slowly, with the 1959 Red Sox being the last team to erase the color line.

Player defections marked the start of 1947. In May 1946, Jorge and Alfonso Pasquel had announced their intention of revitalizing the existing Mexican League. Not since the Federal League three decades earlier had baseball feared losing its talent, and now huge salaries beckoned. Negro Leaguers had found a new society playing ball outside America. In Mexico, athletes of all colors were welcomed and revered.

One of the first players to abandon ship was Cardinals pitcher Max Lanier. "I wound up being offered a signing bonus of $25,000 and $20,000 a year for five years," he said. "You didn't need to be a brain to see how much more that was than what the Cardinals were payin' me." When the team returned home from an East Coast road swing, Lanier bought a new 1946 Chrysler Windsor and drove teammates Fred Martin and Lou Klein to Mexico City. All three signed, as did some of the bigger names around baseball, players like Sal Maglie and Mickey Owen.

The few Mexican League recruits sent the majors a clear message. In 1946, teams had asked their returning war veterans to play at their prewar salary levels. Ford Frick, then NL president, confirmed that forty-two players would be held at $5,000 or less. When players talked of a union, baseball approved a plan by Marty Marion and Cardinals trainer Doc Weaver to create baseball's first pension. After age fifty, a ten-year veteran would receive $100 monthly.

All teams in the majors shared April 27, 1947, as a day of remembrance. "Babe Ruth Day" was declared in parks everywhere. "The only real game in the world, I think, is baseball," said Ruth, in a brief, unscripted speech before a Yankee Stadium crowd of sixty thousand.

In 1948, baseball's king left his throne. Ruth, his voice riddled with cancer, made a final appearance in uniform on June 13, 1948. Yankee Stadium, celebrating its twenty-fifth birthday, was hosting an old-timers game. The

day belonged to Ruth, however. He walked with a bat (borrowed from Cleveland's Bob Feller) for his cane, told the crowd of his pride in hitting the ballpark's first-ever home run, and then departed the field for the last time.

On July 26, Ruth took his final public bow at the premiere of *The Babe Ruth Story*. Babe was an adviser for the movie, which starred William Bendix. The fifty-three-year-old emaciated icon would die on August 16, 1948, but not before the film was clobbered by negative reviews. Not only did Bendix fail to reproduce Babe's swing, but the Hollywood substitute looked athletically pathetic.

Another sudden-death playoff highlighted the 1948 season, marking only the second time in his-

tory that a tiebreaker was played. Cleveland faced the Red Sox at season's end for the AL pennant. Detroit and Newhouser outdueled Bob Feller and Cleveland on the last day of the season, causing Cleveland and Boston to tie. Truly behind player-manager Lou Boudreau, the Tribe used an 8–3 playoff win to advance to the Series. Boudreau, who led players from both leagues from 1940 to 1949 with 1,578 hits, added 2 hits and 2 homers in the postseason preview. Boudreau was hired in 1942, at age twenty-four. Heel spurs had made him exempt from the draft.

Indians owner Veeck showed guile and showmanship in naming a scrappy infielder as field boss. Just one year earlier, Veeck had broken the Ameri-

On April 27, 1947, commissioner A.B. "Happy" Chandler (second from right) proclaimed the date as "Babe Ruth Day" at Yankee Stadium before a game against the Senators. Emcee and Yankees broadcaster Mel Allen (far left) leads the applause. One year later, after succumbing to cancer, Ruth's body would lie in state within the Yankee Stadium rotunda, to be visited by more than 100,000 mourners.

can League's color gap with the acquisition of Negro Leaguer Larry Doby. In 1948, Leroy "Satchel" Paige joined the Cleveland pitching staff.

His nickname had been given to him at age seven, when Paige worked carrying bags at a railway station. The forty-two-year-old pitcher was nationally known not only through the Negro Leagues, but for barnstorming tours and exhibition games (many against white major leaguers). Cynics thought Paige may have been even older than he claimed and was signed as a sideshow ticket lure. Paige's 6–1 record, assuring the first-place tie, ended questions about his worth.

The Series that year began in a cloud of controversy. With two out in the bottom of the eighth inning of a scoreless duel, Bob Feller spun to pick pinch runner Phil Masi off second base. Covering shortstop Boudreau tagged Masi out by two feet.

However, NL ump Bill Stewart blew the call. Tommy Holmes followed with a single, which would turn Feller's 2-hitter into a 1–0 loss.

Although the Indians finally won in the sixth game, Game Five held the biggest surprise. Some 86,200 fans packed Municipal Stadium to see Cleveland clinch things at home, with Feller on the mound. The "Heater from Van Meter" lasted 6⅓ innings, but coughed up 7 runs in Boston's 11–5 comeback. It would be Feller's last World Series appearance.

In order to be allowed back into the league, Mexican League transplants like Lanier had to sue baseball and its commissioner; the dispute was settled in 1949. Most had strayed less than two years. Jorge Pasquel had accomplished his true goal: Miguel Aleman, a close friend of Pasquel's, received credit for the American infu-

Leroy "Satchel" Paige was more than a sideshow addition to the 1948 Indians. Even though at forty-two years of age he was the oldest rookie in major league history, his 6–1 record assured Cleveland of an AL pennant. Paige's first experience in pro ball dated back to 1924, following his reform school release.

sion of talent in 1946, which aided in his being elected president of Mexico.

In 1949, baseball supplied the movies with more first-class material. James Stewart starred in *The Stratton Story*, a retelling of pitcher Monty Stratton's short-lived career. Unlike the Ruth cinematic fiasco, this movie won an Academy Award for best original story.

Real-life drama continued in Brooklyn as more Negro Leaguers excelled with the team. Don Newcombe was named Rookie of the Year on the strength of a 17–8 record and 5 league-leading shutouts. Although the six-foot-four-inch 220-

pounder had begun pro ball just a year earlier with the Newark Eagles, other Negro Leaguers were coming to the majors as veterans. Catcher Roy Campanella, also signed in 1946, was an eight-year Negro League veteran before debuting in 1948.

Entering the 1949 World Series, the Yankees and the Dodgers seemed evenly matched. First-year manager Charles Dillon "Casey" Stengel and sixty-year-old Leo Durocher successor Burt Shotton had guided their squads to identical 97–57 marks. Each had won the pennant by 1 game.

So how did the AL half of these "twins" prosper in only 5 games? The Series took on an all-busi-

Charles "Casey" Stengel's first managerial job came in the 1925 Eastern League. Seen here during Game Three of the 1949 World Series, "The Old Professor" was enjoying a string of five consecutive AL pennants. Fans loved Stengel first for his winning and subsequently for his fractured language, dubbed by sportswriters as "Stengelese."

Brooklyn's Ebbets Field would witness more history during the All-Star Game on July 12, 1949. Roy Campanella, Cleveland's Larry Doby (the first black American Leaguer), Don Newcombe, and Jackie Robinson (from left to right) comprised the first four black players ever selected for the Midseason Classic.

ness tone in the opener, when Newcombe lost, 1–0, on a Henrich homer. A 3-run rally in Game Three keyed on a pinch-hit single by ancient castoff Johnny Mize gave the Yankees their second win. Finally, the third clutch relief appearance by Joe Page, who gave the Yanks a win and a save, sealed the

title. Platooning, pinchhitting, and an active bullpen were just three strategies that Stengel would rely on in the future.

The Yankees were on the move, preparing another dynasty for the coming decade. However, much of baseball would soon be on the move.

1950–1959

Calling the 1950s the "Decade of New York Baseball" tells only part of the story. Of the twenty teams engaged in World Series battles during the fifties, all but six were based in the Big Apple. Yet domination by the Yankees, the Brooklyn Dodgers, and the New York Giants was only the beginning of baseball's postwar positionings.

Liberal infusions of youth would tilt the power balance at the beginning of the decade away from the National League. Philadelphia's "Whiz Kids" nickname was appropriate for the entire roster, right up to the skipper. "The biggest thing in my baseball life was winning the pennant on the last day of the season. To be a coach on a National League championship was quite a thrill," remembered Robert "Maje" McDonnell. Despite having no playing experience in the big leagues, McDonnell became a Phillies coach in 1948, at the age of twenty-eight.

McDonnell witnessed his club's dethroning of the Dodgers on the last day of the season. With Brooklyn behind by 1 game, a Phillies loss meant that the teams would tie for the pennant. In a classic matchup, Dodger Don Newcombe and the Phils' Robin Roberts each contended for his twentieth victory. Visiting Philadelphia clinched things with a 4–1 win. Although Dick Sisler's 3-run homer in the tenth provided the victory, the win was assured by center fielder Richie Ashburn.

With no one out, Cal Abrams tried to score from second on a Duke Snider single. Ashburn's cannon arm out-gunned the runner's legs by an easy ten feet. The four-time all-star would remain with the Phils through 1959, winning two batting titles, and leading all major leaguers in the 1950s, with a total of 1,875 hits. Still, he would be remembered most for the one throw that kept the club's pennant fires burning.

Despite the presence of Roberts, another pitching star sparkled for the 1950 Phillies. "He looked more like a professor than a baseball player. He was unusual," Andy Seminick once described bespectacled battery mate Casimir James "Jim" Konstanty. The palm baller set an NL record with 74 relief appearances amid 16

OPPOSITE: *Edwin "Duke" Snider shakes the hand of manager Charlie Dressen while rounding third after his 2-run sixth-inning homer in Game One of the 1952 World Series at Ebbets Field versus the Yankees. As New Yorkers debated whether their Giants, Yankees, or Dodgers were better, talk evolved into finding which team had the best center fielder. Brooklynites would put Snider up against Willie Mays or Mickey Mantle any day.*

victories and a league-best 22 saves, winning NL Most Valuable Player honors. In fact, he outdistanced batting champ Stan Musial in the balloting by more than a hundred votes.

The defending Yankees eliminated all surprise in the 1950 AL race, edging the Tigers by 3 games. Their repeat was assured by lefty Ed "Whitey" Ford (who avoided using his nickname in early years to satisfy more autograph seekers faster), who was called up in late July, winning 9 consecutive starts.

Yankees manager Casey Stengel admired Ford's confidence, describing him as "my banty rooster." At five feet ten inches and 178 pounds, the lefty was anything but birdlike. Ford, also nicknamed "The Chairman of the Board," became the rotation's workhorse throughout the fifties, winning in double digits yearly after his return from a two-year military hitch in 1951–1952.

Hints about a shakeup in baseball came in 1951, when commissioner Albert "Happy" Chandler was ousted in a forced resignation. Proving again that he was no puppet for owners to manipulate, Chandler demanded investigations over rumored gambling by owners. He spoke out for a minimum salary of $5,000 for players and assisted the players' association in finding financing for the new pension fund. Although Chandler had defended the reserve clause early on, owners doubted

his resolve. His willingness to fight in court with suspended players who had jumped to the Mexican League could have brought about a speedy ruling overturning baseball's antitrust exemption.

NL president Ford Frick ascended to commissioner, a roost he would rule through the mid-1960s. He had risen through baseball's ranks in the 1930s, first ghostwriting articles and a book for Babe Ruth, and later supervising NL publicity. "Baseball is a public trust, not merely a money-making industry," he once proclaimed. However, as baseball's third commissioner, Frick was an inbred solution who wouldn't tip the sport's balance of fiscal power.

Each league welcomed a rookie sensation in 1951. The Yankees found a successor to center fielder DiMaggio in Mickey Mantle, a converted shortstop. Dubbed "The Commerce Comet" for his Oklahoma hometown, Mantle batted .267 and racked up 13 homeruns and 65 RBI during his 96 rookie games.

RIGHT: *On March 1, 1952, Willie Mays made his only prolonged appearance for the Giants in Phoenix, during spring training. The 1951 Rookie of the Year would spend two years in the U.S. Army before becoming the foundation of the New York outfield.*

BELOW: *Joe DiMaggio (left), Mickey Mantle (center), and Ted Williams were facing odd stages in their careers when this photo was taken in 1951. The '51 campaign would be DiMaggio's end and Mantle's beginning. Williams, meanwhile, would see his career interrupted once again. In 1952 and 1953, Williams would face repeat military duty during the Korean conflict.*

Across town, the Giants unveiled their own outfield addition that May. Willie Mays was the king of the American Association, batting .474 prior to his promotion. After beginning in the bigs with a 1-for-38 streak, the bawling rookie supposedly squeaked to manager Leo Durocher, "Mister Leo, I can't hit up here." The skipper ignored the request to be sent back down, and he stuck with Mays, who ended the season with 20 four-baggers and a .274 mark.

Interestingly, Mays was the runaway winner of NL Rookie of the Year balloting, receiving eighteen of two dozen votes. His AL counterpart was Yankees infielder Gil McDougald, whose totals were .306 with 14 home runs and 63 RBI, all the while shuttling between work at second and third base. Mantle wasn't a major consideration in voting, with eleven of the twenty-four total votes going to Minnie Minoso.

With Mays, the Giants won 37 of their last 44 games to tie the Dodgers for first place. A 3-game playoff ensued, beginning with an opening Giants 3–1 win fueled by a 2-run Bobby Thomson homer. Game Two featured a 10–0 Dodgers blowout.

SEEING BASEBALL ON THE RADIO

As Told by Ray Medeiros

Growing up in Fall River, Massachusetts, I could pick up five broadcasts regularly: the Red Sox, Yankees, Boston Braves, Brooklyn Dodgers, and New York Giants. It was a feast for a fan.

In the 1930s and early 1940s, few families could afford more than one radio. It was the entertainment center for the house. If my mom wanted to listen, I was out of business. She had no interest in baseball. Transistors were unheard of. I saw my first transistor radio when I was in the military in Spain in 1962.

In a city filled with tenements, in a summer before air conditioning, you heard everyone's programs. It wasn't uncommon to walk down the street and listen to the same baseball game from block to block. You'd hear radio game broadcasts coming out of small shops, and from barber shops or businesses with male proprietors, without exception.

It was easy to hear who was a Yankees or a Red Sox fan. One old guy in town loved the Red Sox and would sit with his ear against the radio. Back then, you might run your radio aerial up the chimney or throw it over a tree limb, for better reception. That exposed wire could get struck by lightning, which could carry the voltage. During a storm, this man's radio antenna got hit. He came staggering outside, his face blackened with soot, yelling, "My radio! My *!@?# radio blew up!"

I remember the announcers and their sponsors. I knew about Atlantic Oil and Narragansett beer, because of the Red Sox. As a kid, I think I heard more recorded-on-wax commercials from New York than from Boston. I remember announcers going through numerous commercial pitches live.

Ballantine Beer and White Owl Cigars saw Mel Allen turn Yankee home runs into "Ballantine Blasts" and "White Owl Wallops." Red Barber turned sponsor plugs into an art form, saluting Dodger homers as "Old Goldies," and promising to roll a carton of the Old Gold cigarettes down the screen from the broadcast booth to home plate as a reward for the slugger.

I ate it all up. Everything they said, I wanted to believe. They seemed like nice people, the beer and cigarette companies, because they were responsible for the games being broadcast.

In 1949, midway through the game Mel Allen introduced Browns announcer Dizzy Dean, who would do an inning. He thanked Allen, telling listeners how much he liked being in New York. "I don't care much for Boston, but New York..." Dean began.

Later that year, Dean was introduced by Jim Britt on a Red Sox broadcast for an inning. He said the same thing in reverse, "I don't care much for New York, but Boston..." I wondered if I was the only kid on the planet who had heard both broadcasts, and figured out what Dean was doing.

I never saw an announcer on the field before a game in the 1940s. Pregame shows weren't standard fare as they are today. I did see someone up in the WHDH radio booth at Fenway and I assumed it was Britt. He was a World War II hero with a crisp voice and dignified delivery. It was a thrill to see the guys, even pictures of them. I'll never forget the anniversary issue of The Sporting News, October 30, 1946. Ads congratulating the paper were taken out by announcers like Harry Caray and Russ Hodges of the Giants, with their pictures included.

Yankee and Red Sox fans would get into it over Mel Allen. He'd become the most excited—Sox fans said, too excited—broadcasting for the Yankees. His was the biggest "homer." We'd hear his "How about that!" a lot. However, I remember clearly that Allen was quick to recognize the skills of opposing players.

Listening to baseball on the radio, I always felt I was there. But you could feel detached. You could do other things without constantly listening. It's worse today. I'm interrupted by the broadcast. I can't pay attention to other activities, because announcers are shouting to make outs as exciting as home runs. Announcers from the past could be trusted by listeners only to emphasize the high points of the game. They knew when to let the fan use his imagination.

For rain delays, a lot of announcers had a pretty good idea of what baseball history was all about. Guys on TV today can't handle anecdotes without cue sheets. But back then something would remind announcers about what happened ten or twenty years ago, and the tales began.

Those were the seeds planted that made me want to learn more about baseball.

○ ○ ○ ○ ○

Medeiros is a baseball historian who lives in Colorado Springs, Colorado.

Walter "Red" Barber was Brooklyn's first play-by-play voice. "The Ol' Redhead" broadcast baseball's first-ever televised game. When the Dodgers abandoned New York, he remained in the East and was adopted by the Yankees.

ABOVE: *A swarm of happy New York Giants descended upon Bobby Thomson on October 3, 1951, after his 3-run homer bested the Brooklyn Dodgers in a special playoff for the NL pennant. Willie Mays (24) was waiting on deck prior to Thomson's "Shot Heard 'Round the World." Giants announcer Russ Hodges screamed across the airwaves: "The Giants win the pennant! The Giants win the pennant! The Giants win the pennant!"*

RIGHT: *Ill-fated Brooklyn Dodgers pitcher Ralph Branca warms up during 1951 spring training. Never could he imagine being so close—and yet so far—from the World Series seven months later.*

The Giants turned to their homer hero again in the deciding contest, and were not disappointed by the third baseman–turned-outfielder who was born in Glasgow, Scotland. A 3-run Thomson homer off hard-luck reliever Ralph Branca became the "Shot Heard 'Round the World."

The 1952 season began without a baseball institution. Joe DiMaggio turned down a $100,000 contract. "I no longer have it, and when baseball is no longer fun, it is no longer a game," was his explanation.

The Korean War was robbing baseball of the services of many others, notably Mays and Ted Williams. However, "bonus babies" helped plug roster slots. Teams were breaking piggy banks to snare young talent. Some of the biggest gambles yielded the largest payoffs, as evidenced by Detroit's $55,000 inking of Harvey Kuenn, and Pittsburgh's

$30,000 signing bonus to Duke University star Dick Groat.

One of the year's most unpredictable rookies was Boston's Jimmy Piersall. The Red Sox tried to convert the outfielder into a shortstop. Before the season, he endured a nervous breakdown. Piersall's rebound to two-time all-star status was documented later that decade in his book and subsequent movie *Fear Strikes Out.*

In the National League, Joe Black pitched his way to Rookie of the Year accolades and a niche in baseball history. Along with 15 wins and a 2.15 ERA, Black was credited by statistician Alan Roth with 15 "saves." Not until 1969 would the idea be adopted as an official stat, encouraging historians to award saves for past years, too.

Not only did Black help the fifties evolution of the "relief ace," but he became

the first black player in history to win a World Series game. Brooklyn manager Charlie Dressen made him a surprise starter in Game One.

When the Boston Braves transferred to Milwaukee after a March 18, 1953, announcement, the move marked the first time in a half-century that a franchise had switched cities. Still, no one could argue with the move after the Braves drew only 281,000 fans in 1952. Boston's move was the first of four that decade in which a team abandoned what fans had considered to be its permanent home.

The Braves' relocation was an instant hit all around. The team finished in second place with 92 wins, its best showing in forty years. Although their new County Stadium wasn't completed in their first season (because of steel shortages from the Korean War), the Braves still carved out an NL attendance record of 1,826,397.

Although the Cardinals remained in St. Louis, the team underwent a radical transformation. In February 1953, team owner Fred Saigh was

pressured by other owners to sell the team. He faced an IRS investigation for tax evasion, which resulted in a conviction and time in jail. Beer maker Anheuser-Busch, Inc., took over the team in a joint ownership move, a switch from the days of rule by one person.

One of the new owner group's first missteps was in trying to rename Sportsman's Park "Budweiser Stadium." While the world believed that the Cards were owned by a corporation, one man called the shots. August A. Busch, Jr., known as "Gussie" in St. Louis, reigned over the brewery and the club. When company vice president Dick Meyer told Busch that he was a catcher while in school, the executive was made Cardinals general manager by default. In his autobiography, Harry Caray claimed that the eccentric Redbird ruler once offered to fire general manager Bing Devine to give the job to his drinking-buddy announcer.

Surprisingly, the big-money infusion for the Cards didn't produce a contender. From 1953 through 1959, St. Louis never posted better than a

EVEN BEFORE DODGERS, LOS ANGELES KNEW BASEBALL
As Told by Charlie Seaver

We had our little touch of the majors here in Los Angeles, even before the Dodgers. I saw my first big league game in 1952, an exhibition with the Yankees.

It was at Wrigley Field, the Pacific Coast League ballpark where the Los Angeles Angels played. The clubhouse was upstairs from the dugout. Joe DiMaggio came in and played center field for 3 or 4 innings. Then they put in this rookie, some young guy named Mantle. My dad told me, "You've got to watch him. He's going to be great." Sure enough, he hit a home run that day.

I was happy with the PCL. My main memories were of the L.A. Angels. The Seattle Rainiers came down for spring training. I had stars almost in my own backyard, training at Patz Field, which was built for a Rotary Summer League. For spring training, the teams were all around: at Brookside Park, the Browns at Olive Park in Burbank, the White Sox and the Pirates nearby.

I was there for the first Los Angeles Dodgers home game in the Coliseum. Sitting in right field foul territory, we were way up. Only about a quarter-mile away, we could see them moving around, but you couldn't see any faces.

The only way to get a good seat in the Coliseum was to sneak down. As a fan, I didn't think the Coliseum was much of a baseball field. With the short left field screen, it just wasn't baseball. It just wasn't right.

I'd rather go to Dodger Stadium. I still see about 10 Dodger games every year. I have Angels season tickets, but I never go, I sell them. The Dodgers' ballpark looks as new as the day they

opened. You can go and feel like you're at a ball game. At Anaheim Stadium, you feel like you're watching a show.

The Dodgers have succeeded in Los Angeles because they've always been a community-oriented organization. They're very involved. Through the parks and recreation departments, they've conducted free baseball clinics. At clinics, they always gave out Coke-identified postcards of the players and they autograph all of them.

I remember the souvenirs at Dodger Stadium. Danny Goodman, who headed the team's merchandising and promotional efforts, had done the same thing in his previous job with the PCL's Hollywood Stars. He was an avid entrepreneur. Dodgers pennants, programs, picture packs, postcards—you would see it all. I must have driven our mailman crazy, writing teams for rosters, decals, and other free stuff. The Dodgers always answered.

I admit I've lost some love for baseball. Player attitudes about charging for autographs upset me. But for the nostalgia, I'd rather watch the Dodgers play than anyone else. I still remember the Giants-Dodgers rivalry, when I couldn't wait to get home from work to tune in the game with Vin Scully and Jerry Doggett.

I never felt the Dodgers were transplants. I felt bad we lost the PCL. I never felt the big guys ran the little guys out. I never blamed the Dodgers. And I didn't feel bad they left Brooklyn.

○ ○ ○ ○ ○

Seaver deals in sports collectibles in Cerritos, California.

A Baltimore schoolboy named Al Kaline signed a $30,000 contract with the Tigers. Sporting his new uniform upon joining the team in Philadelphia, Kaline would become a star without a day of minor league experience.

second-place finish (in 1957), earning only two winning records under the new, sudsy regime.

Likewise, competitive balance among teams seemed unattainable. While the New York troika seemed capable of locking up the decade's pennants, also-rans were hardly even running. The 1952 Pirates, despite collecting Ralph Kiner's league-leading 37 home runs, finished with a 42–112 record. Their general manager was Branch Rickey who had been dismissed by Brooklyn after the 1950 season.

The effect of the Korean War on baseball was similar to that of World War II, but not as extreme. Although fewer big leaguers were affected, fans again asked "What if?" about young Mays delaying his career and about Williams

coming back to Boston after a second tour of duty as a U.S. Marine Corps pilot.

Speculation spread when Williams coauthored "Parting Shots," an article in the *Saturday Evening Post* in April 1954. He announced that his retirement would come at the end of the season. "I'll be thirty-six in August and, as ballplayers' ages go, an 'old man.' How many men of that age, other than pitchers, are playing regularly in the majors?" Williams added that he intended to retire after 1953, until he realized that his five seasons away in the military had cost him an estimated $500,000 in salary and endorsements. In the end, Williams wouldn't say goodbye until after the 1960 season.

The decade's lowest attendance was drawn by the St. Louis American Browns in 1950, a sorry 247,131. Baltimore offered a room of their own, instead of sharing quarters with the Cardinals, in the form of three-year-old Memorial Stadium and the Browns accepted.

Before Veeck sold the team to a Baltimore contingent, he reached new promotional heights in trying to save his wobbly financial franchise. He brought forty-something pitcher Satchel Paige out of retirement. Paige climbed to a 12–10 record with 10 saves in 1952, adding 11 saves the following season. Also in 1951, Veeck signed three-foot-seven-inch, 65-pound Eddie Gaedel as a pinch hitter. Despite being walked on 4 pitches, Gaedel ended his career the next day when commissioner Frick declared midgets ineligible for the majors.

Talk in baseball's "Hot Stove League" generated a special kind of heat after January 14, 1954. Although "Joltin' Joe" DiMaggio had not been in sports-page headlines for two years, he rebounded, this time to front-page news: the former Yankee married actress Marilyn Monroe in a San Francisco civil service.

The 1954 Tigers sported the circuit's most ballyhooed newcomer. Baltimore-bred high schooler Al Kaline was a $30,000 bonus baby, who turned over the entire bounty to his blue-collar parents. Rules stated that anyone with a signing bonus over $6,000 must spend his first two years with his major league team or risk be-

ing drafted by another club. One year later, Kaline's .340 average made the twenty-year-old the youngest batting champion ever.

Only days before the start of the 1954 season, Enos Slaughter was swapped to the Yankees for outfielder Bill Virdon, pitcher Mel Wright, and a minor leaguer. A Cardinal folk hero from two World Series, the North Carolinian once said, "I'll never quit. They'll have to tear my uniform off." Now, he met reporters with tears streaming. "This is the biggest shock of my life," he sobbed. Years later, Slaughter described the scene:

That's when I found out what a cold and heartless game baseball really could be. Just because I was pushing thirty-eight, the team that I felt was a part of me had decided I was washed up. "I'll still be playing in the major leagues when all these other fellows on the Cardinals are gone," I told [general manager Dick] Meyer.

The words proved true. When Slaughter retired after 11 games with the 1959 Braves, only Musial remained with St. Louis.

In 1954, the Indians snapped a five-year string of Yankees World Series titles. In fact, New York was obliterated by Cleveland's record 111 wins during the regular season.

Marilyn Monroe and Joe DiMaggio, shown here dining at El Morocco on September 12, 1954, captivated the sports and entertainment worlds with their brief union. The couple had been married eight months earlier at San Francisco City Hall.

As Missouri lost one team, it gained another. The Philadelphia Athletics were no more after 1954. Arnold Johnson, who purchased Yankee Stadium in 1953, bought the team from Connie Mack's sons. Although Johnson was from Chicago, he situated the team in Kansas City for 1955.

Johnson's connections with the Yankees would not end before his death in March 1960. Cynical fans claimed that Kansas City served as a farm team for the Yanks, who plundered away all the K.C. talent, culminating with a 1959 transaction for future home run king Roger Maris.

Brooklyn's talent couldn't be stopped in 1955. The Dodgers center fielder, Edwin "Duke" Snider, won the league RBI title (136). New Yorkers could see rising stars in Mantle and Mays, as well as an all-star at the top of his game in Snider. He finished the fifties as baseball's ten-year leader in homers (326) and RBI (1,031).

Surprisingly, a left-hander with a losing 9–10 record became the underdog Dodgers savior in the 1955 Series. Two complete-game wins by Johnny Podres, including a 2–0 whitewashing of the Yankees in the seventh game, gave Brooklyn its first World Series crown. Appearing the next day for national television on the *Today* show,

Podres informed his interviewer: "I'd go out there right now and do it again if I had to."

Another near-invisible pitcher would gain the World Series spotlight for the 1956 Yankees. Journeyman Don Larsen, with the 1954 Orioles, "led" the league with a 3–21 record. He was a throw-in as part of an eighteen-player swap between the two clubs.

Although Larsen went 11–5 in the regular season, he bombed out of Game Two, yielding 4 runs in 1⅔ innings. Then, in Game Five, he recorded 27 straight outs (including 7 strikeouts) against the Dodgers, beating Sal Maglie, 2–0. After the perfect game, manager Stengel was asked by a reporter if this was Larsen's best effort ever. "So far," quipped the skipper in classic Stengelese.

One of Frick's most commissionerlike acts for the game came in 1956. He encouraged the Baseball Writers' Association of America to adopt a separate award to honor pitchers, often overlooked in MVP voting. Hence, the Cy Young Award was born, honoring the pitching great who had died the previous year. For more than a decade, only one pitching award was issued without distinction to league affiliation. Surprisingly, the first Cy Young went to 27-game winner Don Newcombe, the winner of that year's MVP.

Stan Musial evades Brooklyn catcher Rube Walker to score the tying run in a game at Ebbets Field on July 26, 1952. Pitcher-turned-umpire Lon Warneke makes the call. Musial would pace the National League with 194 runs scored that season.

In January 1957, Jackie Robinson left the game. He had been shuttled to the New York Giants on December 13, 1956, for Dick Littlefield and $30,000. The deal was canceled when Robinson chose to retire. When he bowed out of baseball, the Phillies, Tigers, and Red Sox had yet to integrate.

Midway through 1957, baseball tasted its oddest scandal in years. Cincinnati fans stuffed All-Star ballot boxes, in hopes of gaining an all-Reds NL starting lineup. Only first baseman Stan Musial overcame the Reds bias, made possible because ballots were made plentifully available in Cincinnati newspapers. Commissioner Frick intervened, yanking Reds Wally Post and Gus Bell from the starting lineup and replacing them with Hank Aaron and Mays. Additionally, Reds shortstop Roy McMillan and third baseman Don Hoak were benched after one at bat each.

The following season, Frick returned all-star voting to the players for the remainder of the decade.

In 1957, the Braves upset the defending champion Yankees in 7 games. Lew Burdette, who relished being accused of throwing a spitball, posted 3 complete games (2 shutouts) in Milwaukee's upset. Not since the 1948 Indians had a non–New York team won the World Series.

If helping the Braves to a title wasn't enough, the right-handed Burdette staked out another bit of baseball history two years later. He posed for his 1959 Topps card wearing a glove on the wrong hand. He immortalized the prank by autographing the cards "Lefty Lew."

The Dodgers and Giants began the 1958 season as Californians, and baseball fans everywhere adjusted. Team standings and results were often incomplete: late-night games in Los Angeles or San Francisco couldn't be reported by East Coast morning papers the next day. Instead of an immediate score, notations such as "late" or "(n)" kept fans in suspense.

With teams bouncing from city to city, fans became convinced that television was killing the game. The notion prevailed that free games on TV kept ticket buyers away, the same scapegoating that had once dogged radio.

Skepticism could also be found in the decade's magazines who were trying to create controversy that the electronic medium of television didn't yet provide. Some of the juiciest headline teasers from the fifties covers of *Street & Smith's Baseball* Magazine included: "Two More Years for DiMaggio?" (1950); "Mathews vs. Ruth" (1954); and "Joe DiMaggio Says: Night Ball Shortens Players' Career" (1956).

Meanwhile, a single issue of *Sport* magazine (June 1957)

REFLECTIONS ON LEAVING BROOKLYN
As Told by Ron Gabriel

I always viewed October 8 as bad. My grandmother died on that date. On October 8, 1956, Don Larsen no-hit us. A year later was the press conference when [Dodgers owner Walter] O'Malley made it official.

We had heard about the team leaving and read about it, but a lot of us thought O'Malley couldn't get away with it. Maybe he'd back out at the last minute.

I was by myself listening to the [press conference on the] radio in my bedroom at the time. It was like a close relative dying. Others may have needed to tell the whole world about what had happened, but I didn't want to talk to anyone about it.

One of the first games I saw at Ebbets Field was in 1948, against the Boston Braves. It was the first time [former Dodger] Pete Reiser played there as an opposing player, and he got a huge ovation. I remember a foul ball landing in front of me, but I hardly got a fingertip on it. The man who caught it let me hold the ball, which I thought was nice. The only foul ball I ever caught at a game was at Ebbets Field in 1956, off the red railing.

One of the most fascinating experiences I ever had was standing in line for World Series tickets. The day they went on sale was a Jewish holiday, so I had to sneak out at 6:30 A.M. I knew my parents would want me in synagogue. But I prayed harder that day than I ever had: I was praying for the Dodgers to win the Series. That was the era of 1955.

In line, you'd never believe some of the characters you'd meet. Some were shooting dice to pass time, but the police didn't seem to bother them. One fellow told me that he had caught Tony Lazzeri's foul ball off Grover Cleveland Alexander in the '26 Series, the near-grand slam that could have won it all for the Yankees.

Ideally in Ebbets Field, I'd want to be sitting behind the Dodger dugout, between home plate and first base. Because, except Duke Snider, they were mostly a right-hand hitting team and you'd face them [when they were batting]. You'd be there when they'd come in between innings.

Before a game, Pee Wee Reese would pace in front of the dugout, then he'd wave his right arm over his head. Red Barber would announce "The Dodgers take the field!" while organist Gladys Gooding would play the team theme song, "Follow the Dodgers." You felt like you were a part of it all.

I sat with Hilda Chester a couple times. Above 33,000 screaming fans, she'd be heard. When Reese came to bat, Hilda screamed above the crowd, "Hey Pee Wee, I love you!" Pee Wee turned to the third-base line and smiled right at her. For a fan, Hilda and her ringing cowbells got a lot of publicity. Schaefer Beer made her two signs to wave, which read "HILDA'S HERE." Hilda made Ethel Merman sound like a whisper.

No matter where you sat at Ebbets, fans were avid. If the Dodgers hit a home run, a stranger was likely to hug you or slap you on the back. That was true among blacks or whites.

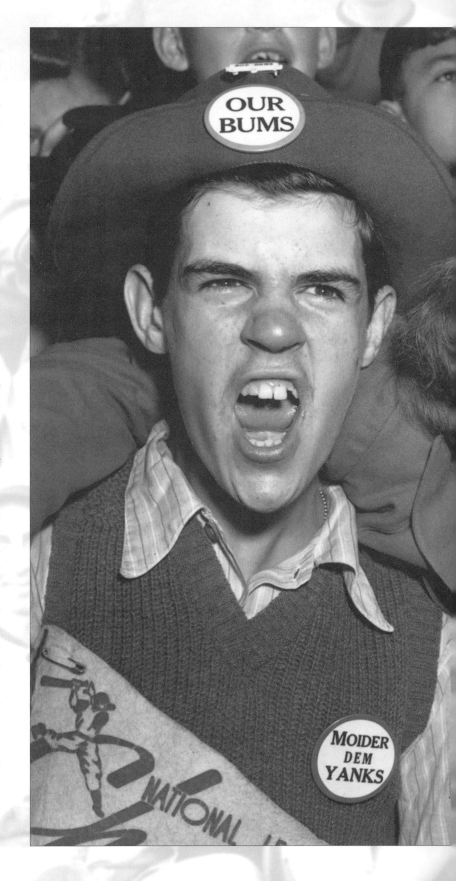

Lots of the players had apartments right in Flatbush. You'd see them in the community, not just at the ballpark. I liked Wayne Belardi, a backup third baseman in 1953. He was doing well, and hit something like 7 homers in a 9-game stretch. I found out where he lived, then waited until he got home from the game to go over. I knocked on his door and asked for an autograph. He must have thought I was crazy, but he was nice. As a kid, I thought his autograph would be more special if I got it on the day he hit a homer.

The fans loved the whole team, clear down to Vin Scully, who was only a third-string announcer in the beginning. I remember Scully backed against a wall outside Ebbets Field, signing for a crowd for thirty to fifty minutes. They'd sign forever. If they ran out of time, we had their cars and license numbers memorized. We'd hand them self-addressed postcards. Maybe we'd toss them in their car windows if nothing else. When they got time, they'd always sign them and mail them back.

Brooklyn wasn't exactly an easy place to live during the fifties. But Ebbets Field was treated like a shrine. There was no vandalism. It was an oasis. No one left until the last out. Regardless of the score, fans would keep screaming to the death.

The team was gone for only eighteen years, but everyone asked me about the Brooklyn Dodgers. That's why I founded the fan club on October 4, 1975, at 3:44 P.M., the twentieth anniversary of the Dodgers' World Series victory.

For me, the club was an escape, like going to Ebbets Field was.

○ ○ ○ ○ ○

Gabriel oversees the Brooklyn Dodgers Fan Club from his home in Chevy Chase, Maryland.

Dodgers fans at Ebbets Field display their raucous cheers before Game Four of the 1949 World Series. When Brooklyn saw its Dodgers head to the West Coast, some mourners said the team's departure robbed the city of its identity.

featured contrasting eyebrow raising articles, "A Ballplayer's Got to Look Out for Himself" by Early Wynn and "The Decline and Fall of the Cubs."

The Yankees avoided a fall after trailing 3 wins to 1 in the 1958 Series against Milwaukee. The Braves remained terrors in the National League, tying the 1959 Dodgers for the pennant before losing a 3-game playoff.

Al Lopez, skipper of the phenomenal 1954 Indians, piloted the 1959 "Go-Go" Sox. The Pale

Hose earned the title with 113 stolen bases, while hitting only 79 homers, the lowest in either league. Off the field, the team was led by Bill Veeck, who wrestled the club's ownership away from the decades-old dominance of the Comiskey family.

If the world wondered whether Californians would embrace their new Dodgers, attendance figures in the 1959 Series quieted such doubts. Comiskey Park bulged with 48,013 fans to mark the Fall Classic's opener. By Game Three, atten-

Tony Kubek (left), Don Larsen (center), and Mickey Mantle celebrate after routing the Braves, 12-3, in Game Three of the 1957 World Series at Milwaukee's County Stadium. A year earlier, Larsen was a postseason immortal, spinning the first perfect game in World Series history.

dance had mushroomed in the bottomless pit known as Los Angeles Coliseum. More than ninety-two thousand fans turned out for each of the three contests played there.

Two wins and 2 saves by reliever Larry Sherry accounted for the Los Angeles title. The West Coast, after enjoying only its second year of major-league representation, was blessed with a world championship. By contrast, Brooklyn fans had needed fifty-five years of patience before sharing in a World Series crown.

The Dodgers practiced packing the Coliseum in May. An exhibition game was held against the Yankees to help with the medical expenses of Roy Campanella, who had become paralyzed after a 1958 auto accident. A total of 92,075 spectators turned out, holding matches aloft in a darkened stadium to honor the wheelchair-bound Campy.

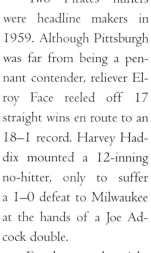

RIGHT: *Brooklyn Dodgers catcher Roy Campanella tosses his mask and goes after a foul ball in a game played on August 30, 1951.*

Two Pirates hurlers were headline makers in 1959. Although Pittsburgh was far from being a pennant contender, reliever Elroy Face reeled off 17 straight wins en route to an 18–1 record. Harvey Haddix mounted a 12-inning no-hitter, only to suffer a 1–0 defeat to Milwaukee at the hands of a Joe Adcock double.

For the second straight year, the Giants were honored with the league's Rookie of the Year. Orlando Cepeda had received the award unanimously in 1958, and teammate Willie "Stretch" McCovey sewed up the honor in 1959 with the same overwhelming vote total.

A rookie pitcher named Bob Gibson, who had played a season with the Harlem Globetrotters, went a modest 3–5 with St. Louis, initiating a chapter of St. Louis lore. But it was another rookie, infielder Elijah "Pumpsie" Green, who completed a chapter in

baseball history on July 21, 1959. Green, followed by pitcher Earl Wilson ten days later, became the first blacks to play for the Red Sox. More than a dozen years after Jackie Robinson, the last team was integrated.

Baseball's shaky structure received a jolt in 1959 when Branch Rickey headed investors of the Continental League and proposed it as the third major league. However, the league existed only on paper. Rickey's pressure resulted in both established leagues appointing committees on August 6 to select a total of eight sites for new teams along with people worthy of ownership.

Numerous transplants, prunings, and readjustments would soon change the look of each league's eight-team family tree. In the decade ahead, baseball would be sprouting in new directions namely expansion teams.

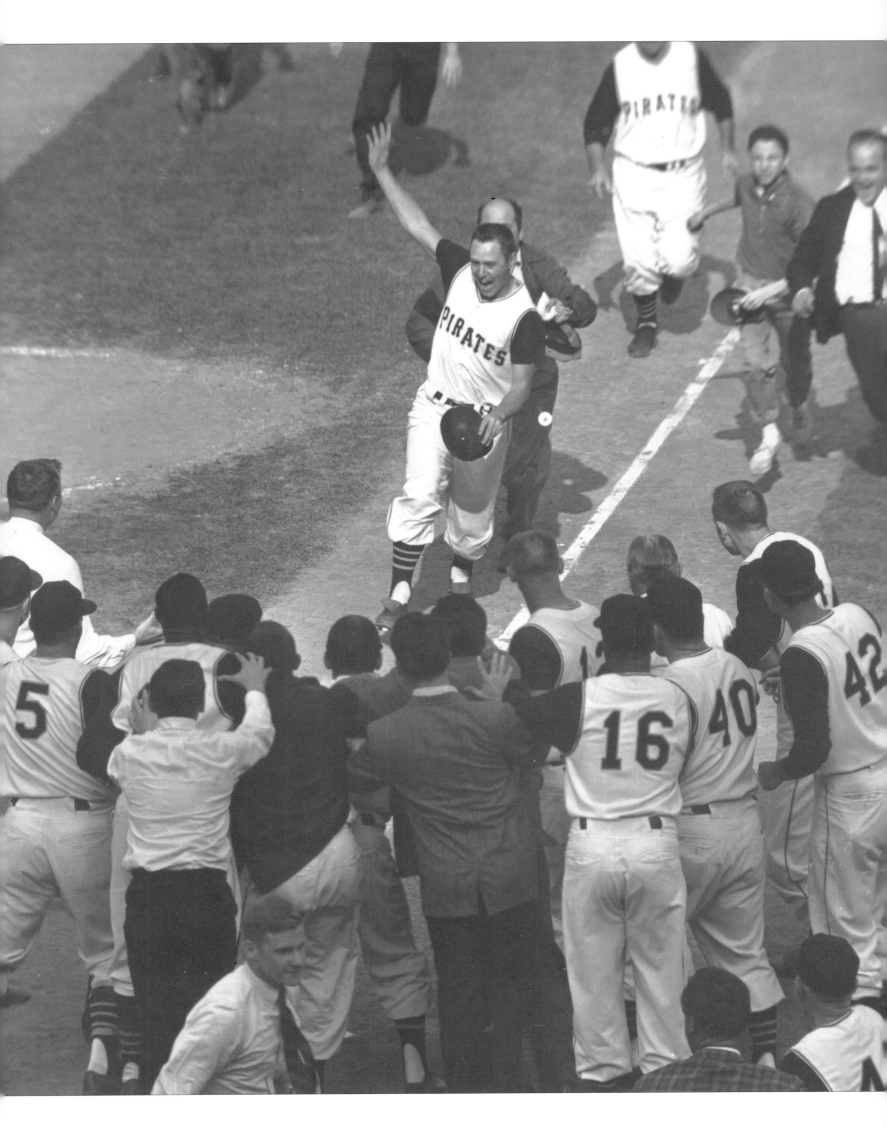

CHAPTER EIGHT
1960–1969

Baseball was getting bigger. Again.

By the end of the sixties, eight more teams would join the majors, giving fans two dozen clubs to root for. As new teams and moving franchises scrambled for places to compete, baseball would become a mix of new, old, and odd stadiums.

In February 1960, Ebbets Field was demolished. A ceremony marked the event. Lucy Monroe, who had sung "The Star-Spangled Banner" at many Brooklyn games, performed the anthem one last time. Former Dodgers attended the event, watching as a wrecking ball painted like a baseball began the end with a slashing drop through the roof of what had been the visitors' dugout.

Candlestick Park opened on April 12 in San Francisco. The bayside ballpark was a curious place to see baseball. During the early innings of night games as twilight fell, fans sitting on the now-shady third-base side would huddle in jackets to brave the ocean winds. Meanwhile, fans in their shirtsleeves sitting on the first-base line would appear to be in another hemisphere.

Boston lost more than the AL pennant in 1960. Ted Williams had announced his actual retirement. In the last home game of the year at Fenway Park, "The Splendid Splinter" collected his 521st homer off Baltimore's Jack Fisher. The shot gave Boston a 5–4 victory. Williams never came out of the dugout to tip his cap because of the abuse that he felt had been heaped on him in earlier years by the press.

Although only 10,454 spectators attended the Wednesday afternoon finale, Williams made a pregame speech to the crowd: "In spite of all my differences and disagreements with the 'knights of the keyboards' upstairs, I must say my stay in Boston has been the most wonderful thing in my life. If I were ever asked what I would do if I had to start my baseball career over again, I'd say I would want to play in Boston for the greatest owner in the game and the greatest fans in America." Before the game ended, Williams told the batboy to present owner Tom Yawkey with his bat as a souvenir.

OPPOSITE: *Second baseman Bill Mazeroski is chased around the bases by happy Pittsburgh fans after his game-winning home run off Ralph Terry in the seventh game of the 1960 World Series. Despite being outscored by a 55–27 margin for the entire Series, the Pirates claimed their first world championship since 1925.*

BALLPARKS I HAVE MET AND KNOWN
As Told by Vic Pallos

The first ballpark I ever "saw" was in September 1954. We were staying in the Schenley Hotel in Pittsburgh two blocks away from Forbes Field. I didn't see the Pirates play, but I saw the stadium.

As a nine-year-old, I found a way to get into a large tree beyond the left field wall, much to my grandmother's horror. It must have been at least 25 feet up, and I could peer into the ballpark.

Previously, I had seen Forbes Field only in pictures. In person, it was bigger than big. I noticed the huge expanse in center field. It was 457 feet to deep center, and I saw where the batting cage was stored on the field, just to the left of the flagpole in deep left center. Those triple-decker grandstands weren't common in 1954. They seemed as tall as the Empire State Building.

I would have loved to have been in that tree during the last game of the 1960 World Series. I think Bill Mazeroski's game-winning homer may have been just two trees away.

The first ballpark I ever visited for a game was Wrigley Field in Los Angeles in 1954 for a Pacific Coast League game. I remember the large office tower behind home plate, which stood nine stories high. It could be seen for miles around. Wrigley was in a neighborhood of one- and two-story buildings, with residential buildings on three sides and commercial buildings on the other. The homes were from the teens and twenties, old for Los Angeles.

Homers hit over the left field wall were fun to watch. They would hit the street, then bounce high enough to hit the front yards and porches of facing houses.

When the big-league Angels moved into Wrigley for 1961, the place got a paint job and was spiffed up. But nothing major was changed. What doomed Wrigley, which was torn down in 1965, was being a neighborhood stadium with no parking. In other cities like Chicago or New York, where people were used to taking public transportation, Wrigley could have survived. Not in Los Angeles, where people are so attached to their automobiles.

My first trip to Candlestick Park came in June 1965. If there is a bluer sky at a park other than Candlestick, I've yet to see it. I'll always remember my afternoon visit, with the contrasting wispy clouds blowing in from the bay. At the game's beginning, there wasn't a hot dog wrapper blowing. By 3:30, the wind was a constant 25 to 30 miles per hour, and every ball was an adventure. What delighted me was the bumps and grinds needed to catch a ball.

Because of the large foul territory, I felt removed from the game. And my impression in 1965 was that there wasn't a tremendous effort to keep the park clean.

The view in Dodger Stadium impressed me the most. My favorite time to go there was at a 5 P.M. game start, sitting in either of the two upper decks. The view is tremendous later in the day, seeing the San Gabriel Mountains and the eucalyptus trees.

Probably the most adventurous seats in Dodger Stadium are in the second level behind home plate. It isn't protected by a screen. Foul balls whistle in at 100 miles per hour. Anyone sitting there should be equipped with a glove, shield, or bucket.

I like Jack Murphy Stadium in San Diego. There's a closeness and intimacy. Fans are closer than Pittsburgh, St. Louis, Cincinnati, or other multipurpose parks. I think baseball fans demand more personalities from their stadiums than football fans do. Murphy Stadium is accessible, and your walk from the car to your seats may be the shortest in baseball. I even thought the San Diego Chicken added a great deal to early games there.

In 1974, I saw Royals and Busch Stadiums. I thought the Kansas City ballpark was beautiful, but the field looked like the world's biggest lawn-bowling arena. With the waterfalls, the Astroturf, and perfect scoreboard, Royals Stadium seemed almost surrealistic.

When I saw Busch Stadium, it was a hot summer evening in St. Louis. The humidity was so high that steam rose from the field. It was three hours of sitting in a sauna. Only the upper grandstand had a slight breeze.

I did like the outside environment of Busch Stadium. I liked the architectural connections between the Gateway Arch and the stadium shape. I liked seeing vendors and the proximity of hotels. Growing up in L.A., I wasn't exposed to downtown ballparks.

I've never been as critical as other fans of ballparks. I'm always comparing one place to another, but I try not to let their flaws get in the way of my enjoying the surroundings. I get as big of a kick out of seeing a game in a minor league park. I find something good in every ballpark I go to.

○ ○ ○ ○ ○

Pallos lives in Glendale, California.

Built in 1914 (and first host to a Federal League team called the Chicago Whales), Wrigley Field is the grandfather among National League parks. In 1988, "The Friendly Confines" hosted its first night game. It was the last park to take up night baseball.

The Yankees regained first place in 1960, winning the American League by 8 games. But the Series went to the Pirates, even though they had been outscored in the 7 games, 55–27. The odd outcome was the only excuse needed for New York to discharge manager Casey Stengel, whose age was worrying club brass. "I'll never make the mistake of being seventy again," Stengel informed the press after his firing.

Although the slick-fielding Bill Mazeroski became a Pennsylvania folk hero for his game-winning blast, the team owed a chunk of its championship crown to Roberto Clemente. He was forever battling "Bobby" and other Americanizations of his name imposed by the media, but no name could do justice to the quiet leader who could literally run out from under his cap.

The pride of Puerto Rico had been drafted out of the Dodgers minor league system in 1954 at the urging of Pittsburgh general manager Branch Rickey for $20,000. A year later, he was a Pirates starter.

On October 26, 1960, baseball's winter meetings hinted at what owners had in mind for the game's following decade. Washington Senators owner Calvin Griffith had been wooed for more than a year by Minneapolis supporters hoping to move the team there. Hamms Brewery guaranteed a three-year broadcast contract, which could triple receipts of what sponsors in Washington had offered. Metropolitan Stadium was built in 1956 without a team but with hopes of attracting one. Other owners hated the move, mainly because even a bad team could appease politicians who might move to strip baseball of its antitrust exemption. Therefore, a new Senators team was added to D.C., once Griffith got his approval to relocate.

In 1961, the Washington Senators headed west. Newly named the Twins, they supplied baseball with its top power hitter of the 1960s, Idaho-born Harmon Clayton Killebrew. "Killer" socked 393 homers for the decade, pacing sluggers from either league. Although he wouldn't win the 1961 homer crown, Killebrew did reign over AL sluggers for the next three campaigns.

On a May day in 1964, two Killebrew homers helped defeat the Yankees, 7–4. Earlier that day, the Twin had visited eight-year-old John Guiney in a New York hospital. Guiney was an altar boy who had suffered first-degree burns while lighting candles in church. Killebrew, who had an eight-year-old son of his own, commented "Maybe I'll hit you

Minnesota's Harmon Killebrew unleashes a classic swing against the Yankees on August 5, 1961. Transplanted to the Twin Cities with the rest of the Washington Senators team, Killebrew's 46 homers had him tied for third in the AL long-ball race. The infant Twins finished the year in seventh place at 70–90.

Yankees sluggers Roger Maris (left) and Mickey Mantle ponder power before a doubleheader with the Orioles at Yankee Stadium on July 30, 1961. Maris began the day with a total of 40 homers; Mantle had 39. For the year, the Yanks would finish with a record 240 home runs.

a couple," when the youngster said that he would watch his idol play on television.

The Los Angeles Angels filled the former Pacific Coast League home of the Los Angeles Stars for their first season. The ballpark was named Wrigley Field, designed to reflect the Chicago stadium and honor William Wrigley, owner of the Cubs and the minor league team. Although the new club had a 70–91 record, the team participated in a record. Never before had 248 home runs been hit in one ballpark in one season. With the field's 345-foot power alleys within easy reach, five Angels exceeded the 20-homer plateau.

In 1961, the Athletics were sold by the family of owner Arnold Johnson, who had died in March 1960, but remained in Kansas City. An insurance company magnate, Charles O. Finley, now controled the A's. He was a constant newsmaker with a barrage of promotional stunts, yet he angered team personnel with tightfistedness and backseat managing.

While baseball was expanding, so was the season. For the first time, the schedule would grow from 154 games to 162.

As the Yankees cruised to a pennant with 109 victories, two players were labeled the "M & M" boys: Mickey Mantle and Roger Maris. Through the first half of the season, both men seemed ripe for breaking the single-season homer mark. Mantle bowed out of the race in September with 54 homers, sidelined by a hip abscess and other assorted ailments.

A home crowd of only 23,154 witnessed the record-breaking poke by Maris. The long ball

increased New York's team homer total to a record 240. While a Sacramento restaurateur paid nineteen-year-old fan Sal Durante $5,000 for the famous ball, Maris owned the game-winning RBI in the 1–0 victory, but not much else. Under stress from constant media batterings, Maris found that he was losing bunches of hair throughout the season. Adding insult to injury, commissioner Ford Frick, still famed as Babe Ruth's ghostwriter and confidant from decades past, ruled that a "distinctive mark" would rest in statistics beside the Maris feat, because it wasn't accomplished in the same 154-game span that Ruth had reached 60 four-baggers in. Soon, skeptics would call the 61 homers the "asterisk record." Ironically, Frick was only grandstanding. He had no control over publishers of record books and encyclopedias, which made their own rulings.

Former Yankees manager Casey Stengel wouldn't be out of work or New York for long. The abandoned skipper would adopt a new expansion team called the Mets and make a home in the vacant Polo Grounds. At the end of the first year, the team owned a 40–120 record, the worst of the twentieth century.

Faring better only in the win column was New York's expansion brother, the Houston Colt .45s. Texas was blessed with a franchise, primarily because Rickey had placed the city on his Continental League list. Home base for Houston was Colt Stadium, a mosquito-ridden sweatbox. A year later, humidity caused the team to break tradition, and they became the first to play Sunday games at night. Out of necessity, the stands were fogged with bug-

IOWA FARM BOY GETS HIS OWN TEAM

As Told by Kevin Whitver

When Minnesota received Major League Baseball in 1961, I didn't realize what it meant. I was eight years old at the time. We never went to see games in Kansas City, because Municipal Stadium was in a bad part of town. Chicago and St. Louis were too far, and Milwaukee was out of the question.

Suddenly, baseball was accessible. Metropolitan Stadium was nearby, right on the interstate. It was almost like drive-through baseball. My dad was a Yankee fan. When we got the schedule, he immediately made plans for the Yankees' first appearance, May 2–4.

It was a pilgrimage. We had to go.

We stayed at the Howard Johnson's on Cedar Avenue. You parked at the motel, then walked over. It became a tradition. People did that for twenty years. In the beginning, if you can imagine it, there was free parking in some areas of the Metropolitan Stadium lots.

The first thing I remembered about the stadium was the colored panels on the front. I wasn't surprised that Shea Stadium later had a similar design. Once inside the stadium, what a thrill! We had box seats on the first-base line. A few yards away, I could see Mickey Mantle, Roger Maris, and Whitey Ford standing there. The only way to have a true idea was to be there, to see the uniforms and everything in color.

My father never showed emotion. But when we got there, I could see tears in his eyes. The closest he'd ever been to Yankee Stadium was the radio. I said, "Who's your favorite Yankee?" He said, "Frank Crosetti." He was a Yankee third-base coach then, but Dad remembered him from his playing days.

Before the game, a group made a short presentation to Roger Maris. They had come from his hometown of Fargo, North Dakota, to see him play. Another group from Minneapolis gave something to Yankee Johnny Blanchard for playing back in his hometown.

The crowd was very quiet. I don't remember many people asking for autographs. They were taking in the spectacle of Major League Baseball. There was an interesting mix of urban and rural. You might see a guy in a three-piece suit next to someone in bib overalls.

My dad bought me a Twins cap. I collected the Post cereal cards, but they said "Minneapolis" for Twins players. I thought the cap would have an "M" on it, instead of the "TC" for Twin Cities. The logo was important to me, seeing cartoon Twin players forming the borders of Minnesota, standing just above Iowa.

After the games, we'd sit in our seats and let people exit first. We stayed to see the airplanes go over the stadium. In the upper deck, to the southeast, you could see farmers planting corn and beans. It looked just like Iowa.

We went back four times that first year. I got to see my first shopping mall. We went to Henry's Hamburgers—I had never seen a fast-food franchise before. I didn't know what fast food was. I lived on a farm near Jefferson, Iowa. The nearest neighbors were 2 miles away. Some days, only two cars would go by our house all day, sometimes none.

On the farm, there was nothing besides work. Twins games on the radio, from WHO in Des Moines, became an invaluable source of entertainment. It was comforting. The games were a window to an outside world. In bed at night with a transistor radio, the announcers—Ray Scott, Halsey Hall, and Bob Wolff—made the game come to life. I still remember the radio jingle "We're Gonna Win, Twins!"

The first year, I remember hearing about players from the Twins farm system on the radio. I wondered, why would players waste time working on a farm? At the end of the first year, they were a seventh-place team. They weren't a good team, but they were our team in the upper Midwest.

In 1981, my dad and I saw one of the last series at Metropolitan Stadium before it was closed. We saw the Yankees play once more. It was like 1961; it was virtually the same experience.

We went to the Metrodome opening in 1982. Again, my father had tears in his eyes. This time, he sat there dejected, knowing it would never be the same.

The Twins gave an isolated Iowa farm boy hope to keep going. Could any of those players comprehend that today?

○ ○ ○ ○ ○

Still in Jefferson, Iowa, the Whitver family still follows the Twins.

Upper-deck dwellers in Metropolitan Stadium, which was erected on a former cornfield, could watch nearby farmers at work while the Twins played. Abandoned following the 1981 season, the mammoth "Mall of America" still stands on the land where the team once played.

unique coiled batting stance accurately.

In 1964, the Phillies hung on to first place until the last two weeks of the season. Their 6½-game lead collapsed amid a 10-game losing streak as the Cardinals flew past them.

The Cardinals couldn't replace their superstar immediately, but they hit the jackpot with a trade the following year. On June 15, 1964, the Cards swapped Bobby Shantz, Doug Clemens, and Ernie Broglio to the Cubs for pitchers Jack Spring and Paul Toth, along with future stolen base king Louis Clark Brock.

The transplant helped Brock to bat .348 with 33 steals for his new club. How did he explain the change?

"In Chicago I wasn't too successful," he admitted, "and in the back of my mind I knew there was a chance that any day I'd be sent to the minor leagues. When it turned out that I was instead going to St. Louis, that gave me a new sense of purpose. It was a fresh start, a change of scenery, and I felt I was leaving all my troubles behind."

Brock's feats propelled the Redbirds into the 1964 Series, but it was pitcher Bob Gibson's heroics that brought the team out on top. Gibson's 2 victories in 3 starts were capped by a record 31 strikeouts.

Although the 1964 pennant race was decided by 1 game between the Cards and Reds, the drama wouldn't match the 1965 tension between the Giants and Dodgers. Their battle for first place would become a dogfight, with two players coming to blows.

Pitchers Juan Marichal and Sandy Koufax squared off in the finale of a 4-game matchup. Brushbacks were traded in the first 2 innings. When Koufax refused to brush back Marichal at bat, Dodgers catcher John Roseboro did the job instead. His return throw to the mound contained a message, nicking Marichal's ear.

LEFT: *The Giants became the first major league team to use three brothers in the same game when twenty-one-year-old Jesus (left), Mateo (center), age twenty-four, and Felipe Alou, twenty-nine, all batted in the eighth inning against the Mets at the Polo Grounds on September 11, 1963. None reached first base in the inning as the Mets won, 4–2.*

BELOW: *Omaha native and former Harlem Globetrotter Bob Gibson would earn a modest record of 15–13 in 1962. However, his 1.12 ERA in 1968 would become a record low of the twentieth century.*

repellent spray, and players were drenched with it. For two years, chewed-up, perspiring fans could see the team's under-construction domed stadium beckoning beyond the outfield walls.

Cincinnati harvested the gem of the 1963 rookie crop via second baseman Pete Rose. Rose would gain all but three of the NL Rookie of the Year votes, with two dissenters favoring second baseman Ron Hunt and one choosing Phillies pitcher Ray Culp.

For San Francisco fans in 1963, the old axiom of "you can't tell the players without a scorecard" proved true. That September 10, the Giants lineup featured Felipe, Mateo, and Jesus Alou, the first time in the majors that three brothers had appeared in a game together.

When the 1963 season ended, so did Stan Musial's career. Stan "The Man" stepped down, after making his twenty-fourth all-star appearance and becoming a grandfather. Commissioner Ford Frick, before Musial's last home game, said, "Here stands baseball's happy warrior. Here stands baseball's perfect knight." Later, when a statue outside the Cardinals' new Busch Stadium was dedicated to Musial, Frick's statement was amended to "…perfect warrior." Always gracious, Musial refrained from publicly criticizing the life-size sculpture's inability to depict his

Pete Rose was in the home stretch of his Rookie of the Year season when he posed for this portrait at Wrigley Field on September 15, 1963. The new second baseman helped the Reds to an 86–76 fifth-place finish that year.

Instead of arguing, Marichal smashed Roseboro's head with the bat. A nine-day suspension and a $1,750 fine cost the pitcher and the team: Marichal missed 2 starts, and his team missed the pennant by 2 games.

The high-kicking Dominican's wood wielding overshadowed his success in the sixties as baseball's leading hurler, with 191 victories.

As an example of how team standings could influence individual postseason awards, Dodgers infielder Jim Lefebvre won NL Rookie of the Year honors, with thirteen out of nineteen votes. Future Hall of Famer Joe Morgan would finish a distant second with four votes. Guess whose team won the World Series?

Beginning in 1965, all teams had an equal stake in tomorrow's baseball stars. An amateur free-

agent draft was held for the first time for available talent from high school and college teams. Although the Rickey-formed farm systems of the Cardinals and the Dodgers had helped those teams build deep reserves, clubs with the worst records were getting the first selections.

Outfielder Rick Monday was the first-ever choice in the 1965 draft, signing with the Kansas City A's for a $104,000 bonus.

On December 9, 1965, Branch Rickey died of a heart attack at age eighty-three. Before Rickey went, he gave fans one lasting statement: he coauthored *The American Diamond.* Instead of a conventional biography, "The Mahatma" chose to lay down final edicts. He chose an all-time team of thirty players, wrote on sixteen "immortals" who

COMING OF AGE WITH THE 1960s CARDINALS

As Told by Jim Rygelski

I became a Cardinals fan in 1959, when I was ten years old. The first game I attended was either in 1954 or 1955, when I was five or six years old. We sat in the left field bleachers. I was more concerned about the scoreboard than the game. At that time, a sort of animated Cardinal would fly around the scoreboard whenever something exciting happened.

One of the most memorable games I ever attended at Sportsman's Park was an exhibition before the 1961 season started. The Yankees were in St. Louis. We were in the bleachers to see Mantle play center field. Two drunken yahoos were too, heckling Mantle the whole game. Finally, Mantle turned around to look at them in the stands.

I had started to laugh at them, but my dad said, "Don't laugh like that. First of all, those guys are jerks. Second, no player should be razzed like that, especially one the caliber of Mantle." After the game, we saw Mantle standing outside the locker room talking to fans, looking comfortable in a polo shirt. He looked at me when I asked for an autograph. I was scared he'd say, "You were laughing," but he never did. That's the only autograph I ever asked for as a kid.

As a kid, I was into Stan Musial, Ken Boyer, Bill White, and Curt Flood. I liked Lindy McDaniel, too. He was tall, lanky, and I

admired his windup. Although teams didn't use relief aces as they do today, McDaniel would close out games and preserve victories. Even without a save rule, my perception was that he was successful.

I never thought anything about some of my favorite players being white and others being black. They were just good ballplayers. I grew up in an integrated neighborhood in St. Louis and went to an integrated school.

I remember how, in 1964, the Cardinals blew a game to the Braves in mid-season, falling to a 36–37 record. They won the pennant by winning 46 of their last 67. I remember how our teacher wouldn't let us listen to the World Series on the radio, unlike in some other classes. When Tim McCarver hit a game-winning 3-run homer in Game Five, the classroom next to us went bonkers.

Old Busch Stadium had its charm and character, but the neighborhood had deteriorated and fans were discouraged. We embraced the new ballpark. One of the first games at the new stadium I attended was a Wednesday afternoon "businessman's special" on June 29, 1966, about a month after the team had moved. San Francisco's Juan Marichal opposed a young Nelson Briles. I liked Marichal, so I wanted St. Louis to win without roughing him up. The Cardinals had just gotten Orlando Cepeda. The Cards won 2–1 on Cepeda's upper-deck homer to left.

In 1987, I met Cepeda at a baseball writers' dinner. I asked him if he remembered. He said that he had hit an inside fastball. For his last five to six years in the National League, Cepeda said that Marichal had never given him another pitch like that. Marichal remembered, too.

Granted, the fans could be rough. I remembered seeing Bob Gibson pitch in June 1967. The Giants scored 11 first-inning runs. When Gibson was yanked, the fans cheered derisively at him. So Gibson doffed his cap to the crowd. He was upset with his performance, and with his reception from home fans.

Most of my memories are from games and teams that didn't win the pennant. But the promise and hope kept us coming back. There was a spark that made us believe. We believed every year that the team would win the pennant, while Cubs fans could only hope. I've always been a naive and romantic fan, but I've always felt lucky being a Cardinals fan.

○ ○ ○ ○ ○

Rygelski is a journalist living in St. Louis.

"The Baby Bull," Orlando Cepeda, charged through nine .300 seasons and eight years of 25 or more home runs. With the Cardinals, Cepeda's love of Latin music gave him the tag "Cha-Cha." In spite of his offensive thunder, Cepeda's conflicts with management bounced him through three different organizations in the 1960s.

had made the most significant contributions to the game, and ended with "The Future of the Game," a chapter addressing television, expansion, and other perils facing baseball.

Just as St. Louis was becoming famed for winning the most one-sided trade of the decade, Baltimore came up with a bigger steal in 1966. Pitcher Milt Pappas was swapped for outfielder Frank Robinson. Cincinnati general manager Bill DeWitt explained the trade, saying Robinson was "an old thirty." Old Frank won the Triple Crown, as he led the junior loop in seven offensive categories. After sparking Baltimore's 4-game sweep of the Dodgers in the 1966 Series, Robinson became the first ever to win MVP honors in both leagues.

Down in Houston, the new club found that losing by any other name still stinks. Changing from the Colt .45s to the Astros didn't change their luck.

Sandy Koufax heats up his famous left arm during spring training at Vero Beach, Florida, on March 4, 1963. Seven months later, Koufax would lead the Dodgers in a 4-game sweep over the Yankees in the World Series, avenging his team's postseason torments from the Bronx Bombers a decade earlier.

Nonetheless, the team's ownership made history. The hope of keeping grass growing inside a domed facility turned brown and died. Therefore, the club commissioned Monsanto chemical company in 1966 to install a carpet of synthetic, substitute sod. The result was named after the team: AstroTurf. The original, ill-fated Colt Stadium was razed to create part of the Astrodome parking lot.

Koufax retired after the 1966 season, succumbing to an arthritic elbow at age thirty-one. He explained that he wanted to leave the game when he could "still comb his hair."

The season ended with another shock. The New York Yankees sank to last place just two seasons after owning a pennant. Manager Yogi Berra had been fired immediately after the 1964 World Series. Team broadcaster Red Barber was dismissed for refusing to remain quiet about the acres of empty Yankee Stadium seats during telecasts. Maris was swapped to St. Louis for a little-known third baseman named Charley Smith on December 8. Maris, who lived in Independence, Missouri, would help the Cardinals to two straight pennants.

Although baseball said goodbye to Koufax in 1966, it welcomed another pioneer the same year. Emmett Ashford became baseball's first black umpire. Born in 1914, he had been umping in the minors since 1951. When he debuted in the American League, sportswriter Dick Young asked of the flamboyant, cufflinks-wearing umpire, "How in the hell can a fifty-one-year-old man run that fast?"

In his pioneering book, *Men in Blue: Conversations with Umpires,* Larry Gerlach captured Ashford's philosophy: "It wasn't easy being an umpire, let alone being a Negro umpire. But since the game is the ballplayer's bread and butter, all he wants is for you to make the right calls. He doesn't care if you're white or black, Eskimo or Indian. In turn, I worked like hell. I was an umpire, not a black umpire."

In Cooperstown, on July 25, 1966, Ted Williams gave one of the Hall of Fame's most eloquent acceptance speeches. "I hope that someday the names of Satchel Paige and Josh Gibson can be added as a symbol of the great Negro players who are not here only because they were not

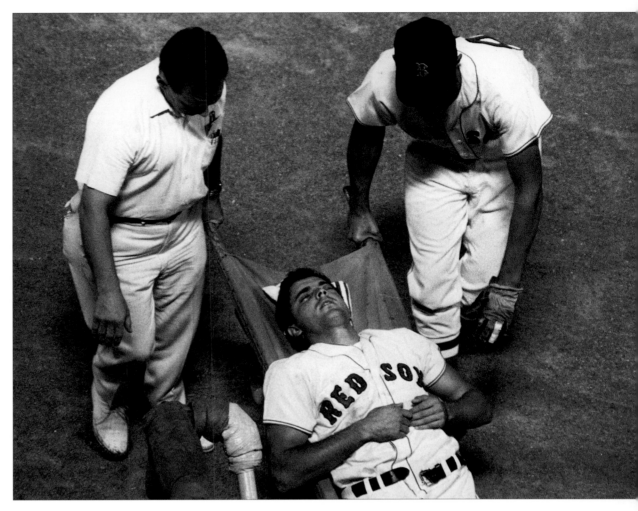

given a chance," he stated. Five years later, the dreams of "Teddy Ballgame" would begin to become reality as Paige was inducted.

Sportswriters called Boston's 1967 pennant the "Impossible Dream." The Red Sox rode to victory on the Triple Crown performance of Carl Yastrzemski.

But Boston faced a near tragedy that August 18. California hurler Jack Hamilton's pitch (questioned as a spitter by some Red Sox) hit Tony Conigliaro under his left eye. Conigliaro had been seen as a rising star ever since he had led the league in home runs in 1965 at the age of twenty. For

more than a year, it was not certain whether his full eyesight would return. Not only would a broken cheekbone keep him out for the season, but the East Boston native wouldn't play full-time again until 1969. Even then, "Tony C" would never hit with quite the same vigor.

The 1967 world champion Cardinals bested the BoSox in a 7-game Series. The team went by the name "El Birdos," a title dreamed up by coach Joe Schultz. First baseman Orlando Cepeda was "Cha-Cha" in St. Louis, a now-happy slugger who arrived via trade in mid-1966. San Francisco managers Herman Franks and Alvin Dark had questioned Cepeda's attitude and his desire to bring a stereo to the clubhouse to share his beloved salsa music. Respecting Cepeda's tastes turned him into the 1967 MVP.

Kansas City lost its franchise following the 1967 season. Finley headed the A's to Oakland, but fans were slow to follow. His move wasn't spontaneous: previously, he had failed trying to relocate the team to Louisville and to Dallas. After finally finding a new home, baseball's oddest owner continued churning out theatrics.

Finley, who once made a mule named after himself the team mascot in Kansas City, put a mechanical rabbit in the Oakland Coliseum to transport new baseballs to umpires. Finley's fondness for

complete games, 280 strikeouts, and a 1.96 ERA. He won MVP honors and the Cy Young Award (unanimously), but gained acclaim with more than fine pitching.

McLain was the son-in-law of Hall of Famer Lou Boudreau. The pitcher was nicknamed "Sky King" for piloting his private aircraft. He played the organ on television in Las Vegas and also released an album.

But in postseason, McLain became a more tame Tiger, winning only 1 of 3 starts. Instead, lefty Mickey Lolich logged 3 complete-game victories to secure the Series. Following the seventh game upset by Detroit, local fans stormed the field. Nearby bartenders granted free drinks for "Tiger Turf," chunks of sod torn from the field.

animals was displayed again when pitcher Jim Hunter debuted in 1965. Feeling that a nickname would enhance the hurler's appeal, Finley christened Hunter "Catfish," inventing a tall tale about Hunter's angling abilities as a youth.

Even without a nickname, pitcher Jim Bunning was the foundation of an otherwise shaky Phillies pitching staff from 1964 through 1967. Philadelphia peddled the Kentucky native to Pittsburgh after 1967, when his three-year streak of 19-win seasons was interrupted with only 17 victories. His 2,019 Ks were only 52 behind Gibson for the decade, ranking as the second-best strikeout artist in all of baseball.

Baseball was treated to its first 30-game winner since Dizzy Dean in 1968. Interestingly, Denny McLain displayed a zaniness that would have rivaled the thirties star.

Detroit rode the wave of pitcher Denny McLain. He racked up a 31–6 mark, including 28

Gibson shared little guilt in the St. Louis setback. Prevailing wisdom figured Gibson would face inevitable humility after his superhuman regular-season stats of 22–9, 268 strikeouts, 28 complete games, and 1.12 ERA. Instead, he set a World Series record of 32 strikeouts, breaking his 31-K showcase from 1964. Amazingly, Gibson has since said that he felt at his physical peak in 1961–1962!

The World Series didn't end the drama of 1968. Reds catcher Johnny Bench

won the Rookie of the Year balloting over Mets pitcher Jerry Koosman, 10½ to 9½ votes.

The stellar seasons of Gibson and McLain, combined with the 58⅔ consecutive innings of shutout baseball pitched by Dodger Don Drysdale, brought about a quick and hasty set of rules changes. The strike zone was tightened, and pitching mounds were reduced from fifteen inches to ten inches.

For the first time in 1969, baseball was realigned into two leagues with two divisions: two "East" and two "West." Commissioner Bowie Kuhn, famed as the NL lawyer who stopped Milwaukee's effort to block the Braves' move to Atlanta in 1966, proclaimed the innovation. A best 3-of-5 playoff would precede the World Series.

Ironically, the added postseason hurdle added little drama before the World Series. The "Miracle Mets" disposed of the Western Division champion Atlanta Braves in 3 straight games. The same sweep came in the AL playoffs, with the Orioles wielding the broom against the best of the West, the Minnesota Twins.

The hope for twice as many pennant races went unfulfilled, too. Minnesota's second-place rivals were Oakland, 9 games back. In only his second season, Reggie Jackson led the league with a .608 slugging percentage and 123 runs scored, achieving what would be career highs of 47 homers and 118 RBI.

Baseball's four new teams in 1969 were the Montreal Expos and the San Diego Padres in the National League, and the Kansas City Royals and the Seattle Pilots in the American. Only the Royals avoided a last-place finish. The NL expansion entries finished with matching 52–110 records.

Just as the favored 1964 Phillies had crashed and burned in their pennant journey, so did the 1969 Cubs. An 8-game losing streak knocked Leo Durocher's Cubbies out of first place for the first time on September 11, never to return. The Mets, meanwhile, won 35 of their last 49. The New

Yorkers imitated the heel-clicking dance that Chicago third baseman Ron Santo unveiled after victories. In Shea Stadium, hecklers taunted the visiting manager with white waving handkerchiefs, singing "Good night, Leo" to the tune of "Good night, ladies."

When the Mets rolled to the 1969 world title, a New York institution was at the helm. Skipper Gil Hodges had been a slugging first baseman for the great 1950s Brooklyn teams. In fact, his 310 homers and 1,001 RBI trailed only teammate Duke Snider as that decade's leader. Not surprisingly, Hodges concluded his playing career with the 1962 expansion Mets.

Initially, Hodges talked about the 1969 Mets finishing in third place, or with a .500 record. Tom Seaver gave New York an emotional boost with a 1-hitter against Chicago, broken up with 1 out in the ninth on a bloop single by rookie Jim Qualls. Now, after trading all position players except Tommie Agee, Cleon Jones, and Bud Harrelson, Hodges had given a seven-year-old expansion team its first championship.

The real "miracle" in 1969 was that baseball was celebrating what it chose to be its centennial season, considering the founding of the 1869 Reds to be the start of professional baseball. Through war, economic disaster, and scandal, the sport was unstoppable. To cement the image of the game as an American standard, a red, white, and blue logo was introduced for Major League Baseball, depicting the silhouette of a batter waiting for a pitch.

Fans could read deeper meaning into the new design, which became a common sight on player jersey sleeves. Baseball needed a corporate symbol, just like automobiles, soft drinks, or other products. And the insignia held a player who was nameless and faceless.

In the decade ahead, players would win their autonomy and freedom to choose a team.

The leading magician for the 1969 "Miracle Mets" was hurler Tom Seaver, who boasted a 25–7 record. Turning a once-laughable New York team into world champions earned the pitcher the nickname "Tom Terrific." History still wonders how the Dodgers could draft Seaver from the University of Southern California in 1965 but never offer him a contract.

1970–1979

B aseball's hierarchy was coping with a flood in 1970—not just Curt Flood, who was suing Major League Baseball to escape the lifetime indenturement of the reserve clause, but a flood of resentment from players.

Before the 1969 season began, baseball nearly had its first strike. Only last-minute peacemaking by a new commissioner, with owners relaxing their hold on the pension fund, kept the players playing.

Baseball of the sixties ended in a cloud of doubt when Flood wrote to commissioner Bowie Kuhn on December 24, 1969. "After twelve years in the major leagues, I do not feel that I am a piece of property to be bought and sold irrespective of my wishes," Flood began. The short correspondence asked Kuhn to announce that the outfielder would consider offers from other clubs before agreeing to join the 1970 Phillies, the team the Cardinals had traded him to.

Critics slammed Flood for turning down a salary of $100,000 a year. Although the players' association was supporting his lawsuit, not all players were. Robin Roberts, Carl Yastrzemski, and Willie Mays each doubted Flood openly in the press.

Not surprisingly, Jackie Robinson was one of the first to testify on the player's behalf. Still, the claim that scrapping the reserve clause would ruin "baseball as we know it" rang through courtrooms. Former Supreme Court Justice Arthur Goldberg represented Flood, trying to use antitrust laws to invalidate the trade. Sitting out the season in Denmark drove Flood to the brink of bankruptcy. The 1971 Senators traded Philadelphia for the right to sign Flood. Reluctantly, Flood tried playing for Washington, but the thirty-three-year-old lasted only 13 games.

Appealing up to the Supreme Court on June 6, 1972, Flood lost, 5–3. Baseball, by law, was not considered a monopoly. Therefore, the reserve clause stood.

OPPOSITE: *Curt Flood turned up at the Washington Senators winter baseball camp at St. Petersburg, Florida, on November 19, 1970. Flood sat out the 1970 season as he sued for his contractual freedom while refusing to participate in a trade from the Cardinals to the Phillies. He appeared in just 13 games for the 1971 Senators before retiring. His twelve-year reign in St. Louis as a top-notch center fielder included Gold Glove honors from 1963 through 1969.*

ABOVE: *As a teenager, Bowie Kuhn spent his summers helping run the scoreboard at Washington Senators home games in Griffith Stadium. On February 4, 1969, Kuhn moved from being a New York lawyer to commissioner of baseball.*

"He was a heck of a teammate," Orlando Cepeda remembered of Flood. "I believe he should be in the Hall of Fame. Not only because of his playing ability, but because he was a leader of players. He had the guts to challenge the Supreme Court for his [contractual] rights. Players today are making so much money because of Curt Flood."

Flood wasn't the only one bad-mouthing baseball in the new decade. In 1970, pitcher Jim Bouton redefined player biographies with *Ball Four*. The tell-all book provided a diary of his exploits with the 1969 Seattle Pilots. For the first time, one of baseball's own was revealing off-field secrets of the sport. Bouton wrote that profanity, sex, drugs, and other temptations were all part of the regular season.

Even the Pilots became courtroom fodder. Used-car salesman Alan "Bud" Selig headed an organization founded in Milwaukee in December 1964 called "Teams, Inc.," hoping to replace the Atlanta-bound Braves. The Selig group tried in vain to purchase the White Sox in 1969, after the team played several regular-season games in Milwaukee's County Stadium. A Seattle bankruptcy court awarded the "Pilots" franchise to Selig and his cronies on April 1, 1970, after they offered the highest bid for the team.

At the end of 1972, union leader Marvin Miller squeezed a new basic agreement out of owners. Now, players with ten years of seniority (five of those with the same club) could disapprove a trade. If the rule had existed two years earlier, Flood would never have sued. After all, his primary objection was that he wanted to remain in St. Louis, where his home and family were.

On December 11, 1973, Cubs third baseman Ron Santo was the first to test the new provision. He vetoed a trade to the Angels. What followed was a trade to the White Sox, keeping the veteran at home in Chicago for the last season of his career.

In 1973, AL owners welcomed a new renegade to their ranks. George Steinbrenner bought the Yankees from CBS. Steinbrenner had the same meddling, combative nature as Oakland's Finley; however, "King George" would spend any amount for a winner. Beginning with a $3.75 million, three-year contract for Catfish Hunter in 1975, the Yankees became a constant source of big offers for free agents.

Previously, an arbitrator had freed Hunter from his contract with Oakland after it was found that Finley hadn't made promised payments to an added pension fund for the hurler. Even so, Hunter can't be credited as baseball's first free-agent winner of the seventies.

Pitchers Andy Messersmith and retired Expo Dave McNally were the first to ride the free-agent highway. On December 23, 1975, arbitrator Peter Seitz was the tiebreaking third vote on a three-man panel, ruling that the players were bound through the reserve clause to their old contract for only one year, not forever.

Not since the 1870s had baseball known "revolvers," players who would jump from team to team for more money. Now athletes had negotiated for the legal right to do so. This was but one major change that would permanently alter the face of the game.

The Marvin Miller–led union would flex its muscles quickly. Base-

ABOVE: *On August 19, 1982, Yankees owner George Steinbrenner seemed delighted to tell reporters after a meeting of owners that commissioner Bowie Kuhn's contract hadn't been renewed. Steinbrenner declared that Kuhn had some "soul searching" to do. Kuhn was reluctantly retained by owners who had fought him through the 1970s.*

LEFT: *Roland Hemond (right), White Sox director of player personnel, appeared in December 1973 to announce that Ron Santo (left), a fourteen-year third baseman with the crosstown Cubs, had been acquired in a deal for four players, including pitcher Steve Stone. The Cubs had failed to trade Santo to the California Angels, when Santo was the first in history to invoke a trade veto clause for ten-year vets. Having a say in one's own trade was one of many small advances the player's union would gain in the seventies.*

ball's 1972 season was delayed by thirteen days because of the longest-ever players strike thus far. After 86 postponed games, owners surrendered.

In 1973, the American League unfurled a shocking rule change: the designated hitter. Still worried after 1968's offensive drought that pitching and defense would not sell tickets, owners sought to keep pace with the high-scoring spectacles of pro football and basketball. Yankee Ron Bloomberg, the team's first-round draft pick in 1967, entered the record book as the first ever to occupy the "tenth man" position in the lineup.

The National League refused the idea, making for a messy situation in post-season play. Therefore, the American League became a final resting place for aging sluggers who weren't physically capable of everyday position play. Fans got a last chance to see stars of the 1960s. Cepeda gave the Red Sox 20 homers and

86 RBI. Tony Oliva, a two-time batting champion for Minnesota, had failing knees. Yet he supplied 16 dingers and 92 ribbies.

A's owner Finley wasn't happy with just one change. In 1975, he advocated a similar rule: a designated runner. Finley signed Herb Washington, a collegiate sprinter, as his prototype. His world indoor track records included a time of 5.0 seconds in the fifty-yard dash and 5.8 for the sixty-yard dash. Washington appeared in 92 games as a pinch runner for the Athletics, never batting once. Although he scored 29 runs and stole 29 bases, he was caught stealing 16 times. Dodgers reliever Mike Marshall tarnished Washington's fame in the second game of the World Series. Pinch running for Joe Rudi, after Oakland cut the lead to 3–2, Marshall picked him off. The pitcher used an unusual pickoff move, swiveling clockwise.

After playing in only a dozen games in 1975, Washington was out of baseball, and so was Finley's scheme.

Meanwhile, Marshall was the first reliever to win the Cy Young Award in 1974. After appearing in a record 92 outings in 1973, he broke that mark with 106 appearances (including 13 consecutive games) in 1974. His specialty pitch was a screwball; some members of the press thought that the pitch fit his personality.

Marshall, who wasn't shy about advertising that he had earned three college degrees and hated interviews, often walked away from questions he disliked. He refused all autograph seekers, telling fans that he felt unworthy to give signatures and that parents and teachers, not ballplayers, were more deserving of admiration.

Oakland wrapped up its third straight World Series crown in 1974. The reign wasn't a happy one because of owner Finley's meddling. Manager Dick Williams resigned minutes after leading the A's to a seventh-game win in 1973. Later, he said, "A man can take just so much of Finley." Reggie Jackson assessed the Athletics dynasty by saying, "We had a common bond: everybody hated Charlie Finley."

Labor problems and radical rules weren't the only shocks suffered by baseball. On December 31, 1972, Pittsburgh's thirty-eight-year-old Roberto Clemente died in a plane crash, en route to earthquake victims in Nicaragua during a goodwill mission to deliver relief supplies.

Even baseball's basic looks underwent radical redressing. Beginning in 1970, the Pirates set a trend by abandoning the flannel, button-down uni-

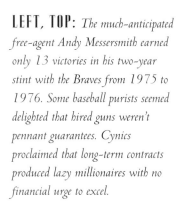

LEFT, TOP: *The much-anticipated free-agent Andy Messersmith earned only 13 victories in his two-year stint with the Braves from 1975 to 1976. Some baseball purists seemed delighted that hired guns weren't pennant guarantees. Cynics proclaimed that long-term contracts produced lazy millionaires with no financial urge to excel.*

LEFT, BOTTOM: *Mike Marshall flopped with the Seattle Pilots but built a reputation as an iron-man relief ace during the 1970s. With the 1974 Dodgers, he appeared in a history-making 106 games and won the NL Cy Young Award. The enigmatic pitcher was known among fans for not signing autographs, stating that teachers and parents were more worthy of hero worship.*

Along with Messersmith, pitcher Dave McNally (pictured) helped players accomplish the goal Curt Flood first chased. An arbitrator discovered that both players toiled without contracts for a year and ended their contractual duty to their former teams. Therefore, the players were eligible for free agency. McNally retired after a partial season with the 1974 Expos, however, making his last victory in baseball a legal one.

form. Double knits with pullover tops and built-in belts were tested. The new styles were cooler and easier to clean. By decade's end, the casual looks and more comfortable fabric would become the norm.

With a quickly changing wardrobe, baseball began preparing for one of its most untouchable records in 1973. However, Hank Aaron ended the year at 713, one homer shy of a tie with the Babe.

Aaron tied Ruth on opening day, 1974. Reds hurler Jack Billingham was the victim. Braves owner Bill Bartholomay demanded that Aaron be benched on the road so that "Bad Henry" could set history and sell tickets in Atlanta. Only commissioner Kuhn's protest reinserted Aaron into the lineup. Billingham was joined in infamy by Dodgers pitcher Al Downing on April 8, the conduit to the record-breaking 715th blow.

Reliever Tom House became a minor hero in Aaron's monumental long ball, slugged before a hometown crowd. The Braves had offered a $25,000 bounty to the fan who caught the famous homer. Instead, the ball sailed into the Atlanta bullpen.

"If I had stood still, the ball would have hit me in the forehead," House remembered. "[Dodgers outfielder] Bill Buckner climbed the fence, but just missed it. I was definitely pumped after I caught it," he added. "After I caught it, a fishnet [from fans in the stands] shot in front of me. All I could think of was getting to home plate to present the ball to Aaron, so I took off running." Teammates quoted the exchange at home plate. "Hammer, here it is!" House proclaimed.

"Thanks, kid," Aaron replied.

Aaron was joined by Lou Brock in 1974 as a conqueror of once-invincible records. Brock stole 118 bases in one season, besting Maury Wills' 1962 mark of 104. For the decade, he registered 551 swipes.

Two homecomings helped close chapters of baseball history in the seventies. The Giants traded Willie Mays to the Mets on May 11, 1972, for reliever Charlie Williams and $50,000. Aaron was shuttled to the Milwaukee Brewers for outfielder Dave May and minor league pitcher Roger Alexander. Mays and Aaron were ending their careers in the cities where they began. Mays called it quits after 1974, and Aaron retired in 1976. Their departures marked the exits of the last two active Negro Leaguers in the majors.

In the 1973 free-agent draft, the San Diego Padres chose fourth. Their selection was Dave Winfield, a star for the University of Minnesota. The St. Paul resident picked a baseball career over several pro basketball offers. The Atlanta Hawks picked him in the fifth round of the NBA draft, while the Utah Stars made him a fourth-rounder in the American Basketball Association draft. Although Winfield had never played football in high school or college, the local Minnesota Vikings also drafted him in the sixteenth round of the NFL

REVVING UP WITH THE BIG RED MACHINE
As Told by Orlando Itin

The first game I ever went to at Riverfront Stadium was the 1970 All-Star game. I was fourteen at the time and a Pete Rose fan. The place was huge, eye-opening. We were high in the red section, four rows from the top of the stadium, and it was hard to tell where foul balls went. Still, we were there. And I got some of the red, white, and blue bunting from the dugout for my collection.

My uncle was a big Reds fan. I went to visit him in Ohio every summer. I lived three hours away from Cincinnati, but listened to a lot of Reds games broadcast on WLW by Joe Nuxhall and Marty Brennaman. I had to. Where I lived in Indiana, there were a lot of White Sox and Cubs fans. Already, I was collecting baseball cards.

[As a teenager] I made friends with Bob Rathgeber, from the Reds public relations department. He helped organize collector shows in the area. He'd help me get good seats, down in the blue section.

We'd go down for Reds games every summer, in a group of eight friends from high school. It was fun to get away from Indiana, and get a couple of motel rooms. They let you drink at age eighteen in Ohio, so that may have made a difference.

For our senior trip, four of us went to spring training in Tampa to follow the Reds. The players were more available to fans. You could stand right next to batting cages for autographs. Players were a little more relaxed.

Part of the fun of going to Cincinnati was going to the official Reds gift shop at the 580 building. There was a waiting list for cracked bats of Reds stars. Because my friends didn't collect, and there was a limit of one bat per person, they'd buy bats for me and I was able to get used game-bats of Joe Morgan, Johnny Bench, and Tony Perez for $20 each.

I was there for the first 2 games of the 1975 World Series. Riverfront was an amazing mix then—kids with their dads,

business people in suits—all people out to have fun. Everyone was crazy for the Reds.

Looking back, I felt that the Big Red Machine began in 1972. Dave Concepcion has been overlooked for his contributions. I think that Cesar Geronimo was the era's unsung hero. Taking a backseat to other regulars, he was a main cog in their offense, but he never made an all-star team.

I never saw players off the field, but I think those Reds players may have been closer to the fans. Current players are off on their own. They look at the game differently. Today, players carry briefcases.

What is my favorite Reds memorabilia? I'd have to say the menus from Johnny Bench's and Rose's restaurants. They mean a lot to me, because I own a restaurant named Bruno's.

Over the years, my affection for the Reds has grown. I'm just glad I haven't had to sit in the red section again!

○ ○ ○ ○ ○

Itin lives in West Lafayette, Indiana.

OPPOSITE: *The magical sight of bats and helmets inside the Cincinnati dugout would later become a bonanza for Reds collectors. Although many teams were strict about recycling equipment through their minor league organization, fans in Cincinnati knew they had a chance of discovering souvenirs from Reds games in the team gift shop.*

ABOVE: *Riverfront Stadium was never considered the pinnacle of baseball's ballparks. Just ask an unlucky person caught in the dizzying "red" section of the facility. In fact, even the Reds seem uncomfortable with their dugout seating, as evidenced by their unusual perches.*

Pittsburgh's Roberto Clemente managed to surpass the hallowed 3,000-hit milestone before his premature death in December 1972. The Hall of Fame dropped its requirement that candidates must be retired for at least five years before being eligible for membership. Admitted in 1973, Clemente was the first Latin American enshrined in Cooperstown.

GIVING FANS A WINDOW TO THE WORLD
As Told by Harry Coyle

I never looked at a game as a fan. If I was seeing a game, it was for work. Yes, I'd be mostly in a truck or control room outside the stadium. But you had to know the ballparks.

Every park was peculiar. For starters, you had to know where you could put your cameras and run cable. You had to know the layout of the park.

I remember the Polo Grounds. It was ridiculous. Center field was over 500 feet, but right field was the shortest anyplace. A lot of stadiums were built for football.

Ebbets Field was a bandbox. The ground level outfield advertisements posed problems. When Gillette sponsored the World Series broadcast and an outfielder was seen catching a fly ball in front of a Gem razor-blade sign, someone wasn't going to be happy. The closest that fans came to equal the Ebbets Field faithful was in Chicago. Dodger fans were active, shall we say. They were intent on being fans.

Today, there's a conformity in ballpark design. For weekly broadcasts, we'd describe the field in the opening. It used to be a novelty to televise baseball. Now, every game in every park is seen. It's to a point where they are grinding it out. For teams seen on TV constantly, Wrigley Field's ivy and the waterfalls in Kansas City aren't mysteries any more.

For rain delays during broadcasts, we'd have "evergreen pieces," taped stories that were undated. They could be aired any time we needed them. Because grounds crews might need fifteen to twenty minutes to get the tarp off the field, we could go back to the studio. Vin Scully was a great announcer

and a great writer. He was very adaptable. Joe Garagiola could talk for hours.

I never liked three [announcers] in a booth. It's too many voices. It's still a gimmick. It's not for covering the game. In the early days of games on television, the announcers with radio backgrounds talked too much. They wouldn't subjugate themselves to the pictures.

NBC's Game of the Week *wasn't really successful. The only reason it survived was that a network had to buy it if it wanted rights to the All-Star game and the World Series. For the Monday night broadcasts, we invited celebrity guest announcers like Danny Kaye in to get ratings. Some of the guests were from outside of baseball, but they were talented and experienced and knew how to speak on the air. If they weren't talkative, you had your regular announcers to turn to.

I calculated that after twenty-five years of directing the World Series, I'd seen enough World Series games that, if you put them all together, they would become the equivalent of a whole season. I was a very fortunate person.

○ ○ ○ ○ ○

Harry Coyle's first involvement in television baseball broadcasts was with the Dumont network in 1947. As NBC-TV staff sports director, Coyle helped pioneer techniques such as offering two images at once via a "split screen." He won four Emmy awards during a four-decade career in television, culminating with the 1988 World Series. Coyle passed away, at seventy-four years of age, on February 16, 1996.

draft. Without a day of minor league seasoning, Winfield would immediately become a big-league starter.

Also in 1973, Kansas City watched a rookie named George Brett hit a puny .125 (5 hits in 13 games), batting at the bottom of the order. Nevertheless, he would become a starting third baseman, winning his first of three batting titles in 1976.

Baseball recorded another first in 1975, when the Cleveland Indians named their first player-manager since Lou Boudreau brought them a world championship in 1948. This candidate, Frank Robinson, was baseball's first black manager. Although Negro League legend John "Buck" O'Neil's one-year coaching stint with the 1962 Cubs made him baseball's first black in that capacity, Robinson's status was a meaningful leap.

The 1975 World Series was arguably the highest postseason drama of the decade. Boston upstaged Oakland in 3 straight AL championship series games. Newcomers Fred Lynn and Jim Rice slugged the Red Sox to the top. Lynn would wind up winning both MVP and Rookie of the Year honors that year.

Cincinnati's "Big Red Machine" fueled up for its third Series appearance in six years. The Reds held a 3-games-to-2 lead in the matchup, but had to wait three days when New England rain postponed Game Six.

The wait was worthwhile, however. In the bottom of the eighth inning, the BoSox faced a 6–3 deficit and Fall Classic elimination. Pinch hitter Bernie Carbo, a former Red, slammed reliever Rawly Eastwick's second pitch into the center field bleachers for a game-tying 3-run blast.

"When I rounded second base," Carbo later recalled, "I told Pete Rose, 'Don't you wish you were that strong?'"

"This is fun," Rose replied with a grin.

The game stretched past midnight, into the twelfth inning. A solo home run by Boston's Carlton Fisk, capped by his waving the ball fair down the left field line, decided the game.

More than seventy million television viewers tuned into the seventh game, a ninth-inning, come-from-behind victory by the Reds. All but the first game had been decided by 1 run.

The Yankees began a run of three consecutive league titles and two world championships in 1976, America's bicentennial year. Bats were emblazoned with liberty bells to commemorate the occasion, while five NL teams (St. Louis, Philadelphia, Pittsburgh, New York, and Cincinnati) added nostalgic, pillbox-style pinstriped caps. A year later, only the Pirates would retain the style.

By 1976, two pitchers had established themselves as baseball's two flashiest characters of the decade. Detroit fans soared to the antics of Mark "Bird" Fidyrich. This flaky moundsman could be seen talking to the baseball, after dropping to his knees to smooth out dirt on the mound. Named 1976 Rookie of the Year with a 19–9 record, Fidyrich never recovered fully from an arm injury the next season. His career would end four years and 10 wins later.

In St. Louis, starters and fans got relief from bullpen ace Al "The Mad Hungarian" Hrabosky. Mediocre as a starter, Hrabosky bloomed as a stopper. Like Fidyrich, Hrabosky choreographed his

RIGHT: *Pete Rose looked like he'd be providing his "Charlie Hustle" show in Cincinnati forever. Rose led the Reds to four World Series appearances in the 1970s. He abandoned the team in 1979, riding the free-agent wave to Philadelphia.*

BELOW: *George Brett began his pro career in 1971, signed by the Royals as a shortstop. Brett debuted with Kansas City in 1973, but looked far from promising with a .125 average in 13 games. A year later, he became a starting third baseman and slugged his club to first-place finishes from 1976 to 1978.*

on-field movements. He'd stalk behind the mound for a moment of self-hypnosis, muttering, nodding, and visualizing each hitter. When he was ready to pitch, Hrabosky would slam the ball into his mitt and march back to the rubber. A cult following in St. Louis ensued, complete with "I Hlove Hrabosky" bumper stickers.

Fans were fuming when Dodgers manager Walter Alston didn't pick Hrabosky for his 1975 All-Star team. The Cardinals announced "Hbanner Day," in which fifty thousand fans displayed signs of protest throughout the stadium. Hrabosky hurled 2 perfect final innings to answer Alston's snub, assuring a 2–1 win on the nationally broadcast NBC *Game of the Week*.

Hrabosky's looks were the talk of baseball in 1977. His Fu Manchu mustache aided his grim visage on the mound. But new manager Vern Rapp banned player facial hair as part of his planned disciplinary regime. The clean-shaven reliever began to falter. "The game is so mental, and they wanted to take away something I was comfortable in," Hrabosky remembered. "It's like asking a combat soldier to go to war without a helmet or rifle."

Before 1977 was complete, one of the game's finest glove men said farewell. Baltimore's Brooks Robinson had redefined third-base excellence, starring at the "hot corner" since 1960. His reputation was built on eighteen straight all-star appearances and sixteen straight Gold Gloves. After his defensive dynamics in the 1970 World Series, Robinson was forever known as "The Vacuum Cleaner" or

"Hoover." When the press informed beaten Red Johnny Bench that Robinson was awarded a new automobile as Series MVP, Bench deadpanned, "The rumor is that the car has an oversized glove compartment."

Following Robinson's 1970 Series fielding display, the Hall of Fame requested that he donate his glove for exhibition. The glove in question wasn't even Brooksie's. He had traded two of his own gloves to reserve outfielder Dave May, liking the fit and feel of the other mitt better.

Expansion mended two fences for baseball in 1977. The Seattle Mariners would soothe wounds after the Pilots abandoned the city for Milwaukee after only one year. Likewise, the Toronto Blue Jays would give a Canadian entry to each league. Toronto had been spurned in 1976, when Labatt's Brewery bought the San Francisco Giants, with baseball delaying the sale until a local buyer was found to keep the team by the bay.

The Atlanta Braves received a radical transformation in 1976, when cable TV baron Ted Turner bought the club. For the first time, cable TV subscribers nationwide could see baseball regularly via satellite, not just via a "Game of the Week" featuring two randomly chosen opponents.

LEFT: *Walter Alston, the only manager the Los Angeles Dodgers had had thus far, retired at the end of the 1976 season. He stepped down with seven pennants and four World Series crowns to his credit. For a twenty-three-year career, Alston skippered the team happily, content with a series of one-year contracts.*

Baseball boasted two of the most colorful onfield flakes during the 1970s. Mark "The Bird" Fidyrich (above) wowed Detroit fans with happy-go-lucky antics while St. Louis crowds loved the drama of reliever Al Hrabosky (left), who faced down opponents with unique facial hair and menacing glares.

GETTING ON BOARD WITH "THE EXPRESS"
As Told by Tom Duino

Nolan Ryan was a star from the get-go with the Angels. People went out of their way to see him. By 1973, he was a huge star.

I was ten when I first saw him pitch. I was there for his third and fourth no-hitters. For the third one, I thought Nolan was throwing especially hard.

For the fourth one, I remember the eye-black he wore, and his called third strike on a change-up against Bobby Grich to end the game. I'll never forget Grich twitching, how he froze. Grich twitched like Paul Blair, whose legs buckled in the 1969 World Series, when he struck out against Ryan. It was amazing to see Nolan's maturity, for him to go to a pitch besides the fastball he'd have confidence in.

I had walked down to seats behind the plate late in the game. I wanted to see this from a different angle. It was worth it. After the game, as Ryan came off the field into a mob of teammates and photographers, I ran behind the dugout and tried to get in the picture.

Things used to be different at Anaheim Stadium. There would be behind-the-scenes stadium tours for fans. I remember being with a tour group under the stands. Nolan walked up from the tunnel to the clubhouse door. When the tour stopped, fans asked him to sign. "Sure," he said.

Part of the pregame tours included walking on a path across the field before games. Once, I passed behind a screen and could see Nolan warming up. We were what seemed like 6 to 8 feet behind the catcher, who had no shin guards on. One ungodly curve snapped straight off the table. How could anyone hit against him? He was amazing. I knew this was the closest I'd ever get to experiencing an opposing batter's perspective of Ryan.

I can talk more about Nolan Ryan as a collector than as a fan. At the end of 1993, I counted about fifty of his autographs in my collection, nearly all of them from the Angel days. My mom was really good about taking us to Angels personal appearances at businesses in the area.

Autographs weren't that big of a deal then. I saw Nolan at an Upland Chevy dealership, with no more than six fans there for signatures. He appeared at a batting cage in the area with no one there for the signing. I brought a Louisville Slugger bat of his to get signed, and Nolan was interested in seeing it. Rick Stelmazek, a backup catcher with the '73 Angels, had gotten bats printed up for the pitchers.

Nolan would sign during batting practice, leaning over the railing. I took a picture of him once. He's there, signing among a sea of outstretched arms.

After the last home game of 1979, I reached through the fence of the player's parking lot to get my last autograph from Nolan as an Angel. He was rushing to his car, and likely knew he wouldn't be coming back [with California] in 1980. Still, he took the time to stop once more. He signed my cap. Looking at the autograph today, it's illegible, compared to his other signatures. No one would know it's Ryan's autograph. But I know.

○ ○ ○ ○ ○

Duino still lives in Orange County, California, waiting for the Angels to win the pennant.

The Angels were blessed in 1971 with one of the most one-sided trades in baseball history. Nolan Ryan, who seemed like a thrown-in afterthought as part of a multiplayer swap with the Mets, suddenly gave California a major gate attraction.

Third baseman Brooks Robinson was an underrated offensive force for the Orioles until his retirement in mid-1977. Known for almost single-handedly defeating the Reds in the 1970 World Series with superb glove and bat work, Robinson made a quick transition to becoming a successful broadcaster.

For starters, Veeck dressed his White Sox in uniforms with Bermuda shorts for a time in 1976. He tried to hire Harry Caray's son, Skip (now a broadcaster for Atlanta). The elder Caray became the ultimate ChiSox fan, sipping beer and broadcasting from the bleachers. On July 12, 1979, Veeck reached a public relations plateau. "Disco Demolition Night" was held, allowing a local disc jockey to blow up old records donated by fans of the supposedly annoying songs.

The game resulted in a home-team forfeit when overwrought fans stormed the fields.

By the decade's conclusion, baseball literature had evolved into the stuff supermarket tabloids were made of. After *Ball Four,* Curt Flood candidly discussed his personal problems in the 1971 book *The Way It Is,* and active players-turned-authors bared all. Reliever Albert "Sparky" Lyle, in his diary of the 1978 Yankees world championship called book *The Bronx Zoo,* added far more than accounts of individual games. He documented clubhouse practical jokes, including his famed stunt of sitting naked on cakes. Lyle complained that after the *Los Angeles Times* ran a full-page article on his nude cake-sitting talent, he quit out of fear that a fan would booby-trap a cake with a needle.

While players were criticized for abandoning team loyalty in favor of free-agent riches, clubs showed the same business acumen. Instead of facing the prospect of seeing potential free agent Rod Carew taken from the Twins without compensation, owner Calvin Griffith swapped the team's sole superstar for four Angels prospects.

ABOVE: *He wasn't pretty and he wasn't sophisticated, but Harry Caray was the beer-swilling, working-class announcer whom the folks in the bleachers loved. Team owner Bill Veeck convinced the mikeman to sing "Take Me Out to the Ballgame" with White Sox fans for the seventh-inning stretch, creating a new Chicago tradition.*

RIGHT: *Albert "Sparky" Lyle was a sinkerball specialist who anchored many Yankees bullpens in the 1970s. Not surprisingly, the tell-all New York press quickly uncovered Lyle's locker-room antics of sitting nude on cakes, giving him fame of another sort.*

Although it took a television-station owner to give the Braves attention, all the White Sox needed was one leather-lunged cheerleader. Harry Caray had been announcing baseball for more than thirty years before joining the 1971 White Sox. In his first radio job with a small station in Joliet, Illinois, the station manager encouraged the budding mikeman to drop his birth name, Carabina, for a shorter substitute. With his midwestern appeal and three decades of Cardinals broadcasts, the veteran announcer was offered an incentive clause. More money came with every 100,000 tickets sold.

When former owner Bill Veeck became the new owner in December 1975, he saw Caray as one more publicity tool. Secretly, he hooked up a public-address microphone to the broadcast booth, to share Harry's normally solitary off-key rendition of "Take Me Out to the Ballgame."

Veeck kept control of the ChiSox through 1980, but wasn't accustomed to free agency. Still, he used Caray and every other promotional gimmick imaginable to draw fans to the games of his lackluster franchise.

end the decade striking out 2,678 batters, the best in baseball.

Pete Rose, baseball's ten-year leader with 2,045 hits, briefly became baseball's top-paid player in December 1978. He fled the Reds to sign a four-year, $3.2 million contract with Philadelphia.

Baseball's decade-long home run leader at 292 was Willie Stargell. The Pittsburgh pounder was nicknamed "Pops" at age thirty-eight. The team captain, a survivor from the 1971 championship, seemed parental in 1979. Stargell passed out gold stars for excellence, and teammates displayed the awards on their caps.

Carew had asked for a trade in 1978, after Griffith spouted a shocking off-the-cuff speech to the Waseca Lions Club in a hamlet outside the Twin Cities. Supposedly, Griffith told the group he had moved his team from Washington because Minnesota had fewer blacks. Griffith swore that the event was supposed to be free of reporters. Also, he admitted to having had a couple of drinks and wanting to be funny. Yet Carew condemned the owner. "The days of Kunta Kinte are over. I refuse to be a slave on his plantation and play for a bigot."

Naturally, Griffith and Carew didn't part as bosom chums. In Carew's 1979 autobiography, he wrote: "I could no longer work for a man like Calvin Griffith. Calvin is a hard-hearted guy who had not admitted to himself that times do actually change. Because of his attitude, the Twins have sunk in the standings and at the gate."

California had engaged in another blockbuster trade to start the decade. On December 10, 1971, shortstop Jim Fregosi was swapped to the New York Mets for Francisco Estrada, Leroy Stanton, Don Rose, and pitcher Nolan Ryan. Ryan would

Pittsburgh adopted the Sister Sledge tune "We Are Family" for their guardian first baseman. The Bucs took a 7-game Series from the Orioles as Stargell contributed a .400 average. He supplied 79 RBI and the club's only 3 homers. Stargell wound up becoming the first co-MVP of the National League, splitting the award with batting champion Keith Hernandez of St. Louis.

Regardless of the records being set, baseball was changing quickly. Not counting the 1976 renovation of Yankee Stadium, six new parks opened: Pittsburgh's Three Rivers Stadium and Cincinnati's Riverfront Stadium in 1970; Philadelphia's Veterans Stadium in 1971; Kansas City's Royals Stadium in 1973; and Seattle's Kingdome and Montreal's Olympic Stadium in 1977. All chose artificial turf.

The clothing was unrecognizable for many teams. Only on Saturdays, the 1979 Phillies wore burgundy tops and bottoms. The Pirates became fashion mavens, sporting five different combinations of jerseys and pants.

In the following decade, baseball would struggle to retain its history and regain its identity.

Pittsburgh pushed the 1970s doubleknit uniform craze to the limit with a series of mix-and-match outfits. No one complained about the attire of sluggers like Willie "Pops" Stargell, though, as he contributed a co-MVP Award to the team's 1979 world championship campaign. More than an offensive leader, Stargell served as a father figure in the clubhouse, passing out gold stars for fine play.

CHAPTER TEN

1980–1989

B aseball faced more labor pains at the start of the 1980s.

Take the case of Padres shortstop Ozzie Smith. The team renewed him at his 1979 salary, so Smith's agent took out a classified ad that read, "Padre player wants part-time employment to supplement income. . .would quit baseball for right opportunity."

Joan Kroc, wife of the team owner, tried to one-up Smith. She told the press that the gardener on their estate needed an assistant. The job would pay $4.50 per hour, but Smith could make a dollar an hour extra because of his college education.

Round two of the media blitz became more comical. Supposedly, Smith was ready to take a leave of absence to ride in the Tour de France for $100,000. The agent didn't tell the press that Smith didn't even ride a bike.

Elsewhere, players were geared up for a strike in 1980. Of 968 union members voting, only Kansas City's team representative voted against the idea. Utility infielder Jerry Terrell said that religious reasons kept him from approving the strike. A last-minute truce limited the dispute to eight days of missed spring training games.

The American League's first season of the new decade ended with George Brett flirting with record keepers. Brett's .390 average won the batting title, becoming the highest mark since Ted Williams batted .406 in 1941.

The 1980 Phillies were world champions, thanks to a procession led by Michael Jack Schmidt. The third baseman would contribute 313 round-trippers in the decade, leading all sluggers. "Mike wants to hit it all the way out of the stadium, not just 330 feet over the outfield fence," shortstop teammate Larry Bowa once said. Of Schmidt's home run capabilities, Bowa added, "With his swing, he can hit 20 accidentally."

OPPOSITE: *Ozzie Smith was far from being "The Wizard of Oz" during his early days as a Padre. The team, despite being owned by the heir to a McDonald's franchise fortune, wasn't keen on Smith's salary demands. After the 1981 season, San Diego swapped its troublesome shortstop to the St. Louis Cardinals for another controversial infielder, Garry Templeton.*

The 1980 unrest disrupted only the tail end of spring training, but the lack of a new basic agreement made a strike inevitable in 1981, blotting out fifty days and more than 700 games. On June 11, players halted the season. Owners made their first stab at a salary cap, with no results. Commissioner Bowie Kuhn tried to salvage the year by creating a split season of pre- and poststrike division leaders, with additional playoffs.

The Cubs lost a team tradition, but maintained a Chicago custom following 1981. Lead broadcaster Jack Brickhouse, a Cubbie tradition for more than four decades, was retiring. Brickhouse was famed for "hey-hey" cheers for homers, double plays, and other team highlights.

At the same time, Harry Caray, who became a cult hero with White Sox followers, walked away from the Pale Hose. New owners Jerry Reinsdorf

and Eddie Einhorn were launching a television subscriber service, making once-free broadcasts of ChiSox games cost money. Worst of all, Caray was offered only a one-year contract.

The Cubs needed a new local hero at the mike, and Caray needed career insurance. He feared being blamed for the White Sox failure after a year of pay-TV and becoming an unemployed "Harry Who?" When Caray and the Cubs collaborated, he was seen (for free) by thirty million households picking up superstation WGN. Even by 1989, the White Sox plan hadn't signed up fifteen thousand subscribers.

Yankees magnate George Steinbrenner became stained early in the decade through an embarrassing transaction with the St. Louis Cardinals. When Dave Winfield joined New York for 1981 (with a ten-year contract worth up to

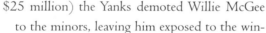

$25 million) the Yanks demoted Willie McGee to the minors, leaving him exposed to the winter minor league draft. Instead of losing McGee to another club, the Cards offered reliever Bob Sykes. Not only did Sykes never pitch for the Yankees, but he never pitched a day in the majors after the trade.

McGee, by contrast, batted .296 with 4 homers, 56 RBI, and 24 steals. Soon, he was nicknamed "E.T." after the movie. Some of the media thought he possessed extra-terrestrial super-speed. Others joked that he looked like the extra-terrestrial.

Probably the biggest losers of 1981 turned out to be the Minnesota Twins. In their last year at Metropolitan Stadium, they drew only 469,090 fans, the smallest turnout of the decade. Not surprisingly, attendance did not go through the roof at the Metrodome, their new home for 1982.

Stadium architects claimed that air conditioning was unnecessary because of the flexible roof.

When sportswriters renamed the new ballpark "The Sweatbox" and fans stayed away, the team threatened to move out. In mid-1983, stadium authorities installed air conditioning.

Cal Ripken, Jr., the eighties equivalent to the Iron Horse, began his Baltimore career in 1982. He nosed out Minnesota first baseman Kent Hrbek for Rookie of the Year honors.

A single-season record, once thought untouchable, was shattered on August 27, 1982. Oakland's Rickey Henderson swiped his 119th base, on the way to 130 steals.

Robin Yount, who began as a teenager with the Brewers in 1975, would switch from shortstop to center field to end the 1980s. However, his bat would remain potent. His 385 votes for league MVP were the most for anyone in the decade. Likewise, Yount's 1,731 hits would rule all batsmen for the decade.

Yount's Brewers yielded to the Cardinals in a 7-game World Series. St. Louis won the contest on the shoulders of a man whose career seemed finished two years earlier.

During spring training with the Royals in 1980, Darrell Porter left camp without notice. He emerged from an Arizona rehabilitation clinic, confessing to previous drug and alcohol addiction. The Cards signed the catcher to a five-year, $3.5 million free agent's deal in 1981,

CAL COLLECTOR COVETS THE MEMORIES OF MEMORABILIA

As Told by Bill Haelig

I was graduating from college in 1983. I was intrigued with an article I read in 1982 about a collector who specialized in Hank Aaron items. I had grown up a Brooks Robinson fan. But after looking at the rising prices of Robinson cards, I decided against that specialty.

I thought, "Maybe I'll start with someone new." When Doug DeCinces was traded, Cal Ripken, Jr., was brought up to replace him at third base. My attitude was, "Once you aren't an Oriole, I have no interest in you." So Cal just happened to be the right person at the right time. Chasing the consecutive game streak had nothing to do with my collecting choice. The fact that he played third base and was the 1982 Rookie of the Year helped.

Ripken's career parallels the growth in the sports-card market. Did you realize that the number of different Cal cards produced in one year could outnumber all the cards Brooks appeared on in his whole career?

I've seen 15 to 20 Oriole games a year since 1984. I found that Ripken would carry autographed colored postcards of himself after games. Outside Memorial Stadium, if he didn't have time to sign for everyone, he'd put someone in the crowd in charge of the pile of postcards. "I've got to run. Make sure everyone gets one," he'd say.

Normally, he'd sign for everyone after games. He even kept more autographed postcards in his car. If a kid wanted him to sign rumpled paper or a hot-dog wrapper, Cal would hand the kid a photo, saying, "Maybe you'd like one of these instead."

In the mid-1980s, when Cal was single, he'd be a guest signer at card shows two or three times a year. I attended a North Jersey show in January 1985, when Cal was appearing with Ron Darling. At the front of the autograph line was a card table filled with equipment Cal had accumulated during the 1984 season. He donated all these items to help raise money for charity. I got a pair of game-used spikes for $50 and added a wristband and a batting glove to my collection. That showed the innocence of the hobby then.

In 1983, Cal's hometown, Havre de Grace, MD, started a small informal fan club. Each year at the local Moose lodge, members would meet and eat off Styrofoam plates. Cal wouldn't be compensated, but he'd come each year, bringing a bag full of memorabilia to raffle. Cal, Sr. and Billy made appearances, too. They'd all sign for free. By 1991, the club had to stop. It lost its innocence. Dealers were beginning to take ad-

vantage. It was too much of a good thing. I attended the last three meetings, but could have kicked myself for not finding out about it sooner.

In 1991, you could count the serious Ripken collectors on one hand. But after 1991, when he won the All-Star game homer hitting contest and won his second AL Most Valuable Player award, more people jumped on board. Like Ryan, collectors were noticing his numbers.

In 1988, I was treated to a media pass for an Orioles game by a sports director for a radio station. After the game, I looked around the Baltimore clubhouse and wondered what would be a neat collectible. After Cal finished doing interviews, I walked over to his locker. Since it was the last home game of the year, I asked if I could have the laminated cardboard nameplate over his locker.

He said, "I don't know. I've got to check."

Throughout the successful drive to play in 2,131 consecutive games, Ripken never stopped giving back to fans before, during, or after games.

He left. I wondered, was he making a fool out of me? Here's the biggest star on the team, who could do almost anything without getting in trouble, but he wanted to get permission to give away a cardboard sign.

But he did come back. "I checked. Yeah, you can have it," he said.

Feeling like the kid who got Mean Joe Greene's jersey on the Coke commercial, I thanked him. Then I went to see his brother Billy across the locker room. Right away, he gave me his nameplate, then said, "Wait. I've got something for you."

Cal Ripken, Sr., was fired as manager after losing the first 6 games of 1988. Billy went from number 3 to number 7 then, saying that he couldn't stand seeing another player wearing his dad's number. Billy dug to the bottom of his locker, and pulled out another nameplate. He hands me "Ripken #3," the nameplate he had started the year with.

I lived 110 miles from the park, and I could have walked all the way home. Those are the kind of things I love, something with a memory attached.

I think we all grew up hoping to play in the majors someday. Well, Cal lives the life we dream about if we turned into a baseball player. Having a father as a coach, making the local team, becoming a star, it's like Hollywood couldn't produce a better script. People can see Cal as their next-door neighbor.

○ ○ ○ ○ ○

Haelig is a commercial insurance underwriter in Blandon, Pennsylvania.

reuniting Porter and his ex–Royals manager, Whitey Herzog.

Porter batted a measly .231 in the regular season, only to assemble 13 hits in 10 postseason games. No one since Willie Stargell in 1979 won MVP awards for both the NL championship series and the World Series.

St. Louis won the World Series with a new shortstop. On February 11, 1982, San Diego's Smith was swapped for Garry Templeton. Templeton's days as a Cardinal were numbered. He derided a jeering home crowd by grabbing his crotch, followed by a middle-finger salute, capping his shaky relationship with manager Herzog. Not only would Smith continue a history-making streak of 13 straight Gold Glove wins, he'd become an opening-day tradition. Trotting out to take his position, "The Wizard of Oz" would provide a running backflip.

The Minnesota Twins faced becoming the Tampa Bay Twins in 1984. Indianapolis, Denver, and Vancouver also bid for the transplantable team. Instead, the Griffith family sold the team to local banker Carl Pohlad. Later, it was revealed that business mogul Donald Trump had tinkered with buying the Twins to move them to New Jersey's Meadowlands Stadium.

Although all-star and postseason plays would be discussed and debated through the decade, the most controversial regular-season game of the eighties came at Yankee Stadium on July 24, 1983. Forever known as the "Pine Tar Incident," the firestorm of argument surrounded George Brett's bat. He used the wand to poke a ninth-inning 2-run homer to win the game. However, a protest by Yankees manager Billy Martin over Brett's illegally applying pine tar too far on the handle over-ruled the homer. A game-concluding out was substituted on appeal, nullifying the home run.

When 1983 ended, so did Carl Yastrzemski's career. The left field successor to Ted Williams spent a final season as designated hitter. Unlike Williams, who never tipped his cap following his last atbat, Yastrzemski gave his cap. In the top of the eighth inning, after "Yaz" took his left field post one final symbolic time, manager Ralph Houk called him back. Before exiting, the Massachusetts native turned in a circle to wave to the entire crowd. He removed his cap, giving it to a boy in the stands.

The day before his departure, Yastrzemski made a speech to the crowd. "New England, I love you!" he proclaimed. In another un-Williamslike

gesture, "Yaz" shook hands with fans behind the first-base stands, then rimmed the stands from jogging box seats to outfield bleachers. Never before had a star player tried to thank every fan personally for their support.

In 1984, Harry Caray screamed to cable TV viewers across America: "The Cubs win the pennant! The Cubs win the pennant! The Cubs win the pennant!" Few people cared that he was borrowing from the 1951 playoff broadcast when Russ Hodges had croaked out the same edict about his Giants. After all, the Cubbies had waited longer, since 1945, for a similar call.

The following season, baseball's remaining superstars began staking out spots in history. Pitchers Tom Seaver, now with the White Sox, and Phil Niekro, who bounced around and finally ended up with the Indians, entered the elite club of 300-game winners. Niekro's achievement was more significant, considering that he tallied triumphs mainly on the strength of his knuckleball. Yankee Bobby Murcer once said, "Trying to hit Phil Niekro is like trying to eat Jell-O with chopsticks. Sometimes you might get a piece, but most of the time you get hungry."

The only man to reach 3,000 career hits in the decade was Rod Carew. On August 4, 1985, the Twin-turned-Angel singled off Minnesota's Frank Viola. "Trying to sneak a pitch past Carew is like trying to sneak a sunrise past a rooster," Catfish Hunter said of the sixteenth man to reach the hallowed offensive mark.

Pete Rose, though, moved from a royal court to the throne of baseball hit king. Back in Cincinnati as a player-manager, he broke Ty Cobb's record at home on September 11, 1985.

Instead of a "subway" series between crosstown rivals, baseball got its first "Show Me" Series. The Cardinals and the Royals heated up Interstate 70 with an all-state matchup. St. Louis, of course, had more baseball history, but the Royals started a new chapter for Missouri baseball with their victory.

Angelo Bartlett Giamatti grew up in South Hadley, Massachusetts. He came to baseball as the president of Yale University, initially a professor of literature. In 1986, he began as president of the National League. When he joined baseball's hierarchy, Giamatti confessed, "The toughest thing about this job is that I will no longer be able to root for the Red Sox."

Despite his professorial experience, mastery of English, and numerous published writings, Giamatti's assessments of baseball always came from his upbringing as a fan. "Americans have become accustomed to associating summer's renewal of the earth and fall's harvest with baseball. You can't conceive of baseball being played in the winter. It is fitted to the season in an extraordinary way." Translation: the commish hoped baseball could continue to be an outdoor game on real grass, free of domes and artificial turf.

Giamatti officially witnessed his Red Sox prepare for another postseason heartbreak in 1986. Boston had ridden to postseason glory on the back of Roger Clemens. The highlight of his 24–4 season was a 3-hitter against the Mariners. In the April 29 complete game, "Rocket Man" struck out a record twenty batters amid 3 hits and no walks. Clemens became the first to collect three awards—the MVP, the Cy Young, and the All-Star MVP—in the same year.

In Game Six, Boston neared its first Series crown since 1918, only 1 strike away from a title. With none on and 2 out in the tenth inning, 3 singles and a wild pitch were climaxed by a Mookie Wilson grounder to BoSox first sacker Bill Buckner. As the ball trickled through Buckner's leg for an error, so did all hope for a world championship.

Kansas City hosted the year's most versatile player. Vincent "Bo" Jackson batted only .207 after becoming a September regular. Actual stats didn't matter to fans who were

Pitchers Tom Seaver (left) and Phil Niekro (below, right) continued their old ways for new employers in the 1980s. Both men would shatter the 300-win barriers during the decade. Their accomplishments would be showcased by new commissioner Bart Giamatti (below, left), a poetic leader who helped communicate the average fan's love of the sport. Unlike players who had spent a lifetime in the game, Giamatti was an academic, a teacher, and an administrator whose concern for the game's history and tradition eclipsed typical worries over team profit.

A BRIEF BUT GLORIOUS CAREER

Dick Howser was an all-star shortstop for the Kansas City Athletics in 1961, his first season, losing the Rookie of the Year award by one vote to Boston pitcher Don Schwall. Howser was a success as a Florida State University collegiate coach, and his big-league managerial debut came with the 1980 Yankees. Despite winning 103 games, his team was beaten by the Royals in 3 straight playoff games. Howser resigned, and returned to his Kansas City roots to manage the Royals in 1981. Following a division title in 1984, Howser's 1985 crew won a world championship. However, he began suffering from headaches and memory loss the following year. On July 18, 1986, news came that Howser suffered from a malignant brain tumor. After having operations, Howser tried to return as K.C. manager in 1987. He died on June 17, 1987, at age fifty. Here, the Royals long-time team announcer remembers a man whom many never had time to know.

As Told by Denny Matthews

If you had seen Dick Howser on TV when he was in the Royals dugout, chances are he was standing still, not doing a thing. Fans may have thought he was quiet, unemotional, and stoic. Just the opposite was true. Howser was fiery and competitive, but no one saw it publicly. Seeing him get into it with umpires may have been the only exception.

The players knew the other side of him, though. The players knew it was there. He never got too fancy with his managing. He let his players play. If he was going to air someone out, he did it behind closed doors.

The players knew what to expect with Dick. He came across to them, communicated with them, so they knew what he expected. They responded. The players knew he wouldn't panic. He wasn't too high after wins or too low after losses. He was right down the middle. "Let's get it done. No excuses," was something he'd always say.

Every year since Whitey Herzog, I've done a five-minute pregame show on radio with the manager. Dick was well-spoken and intelligent. He was a details guy. He was a good interview, without the trite clichés. But he was very secretive about player injuries and wouldn't say much about his plans for opponents. Many managers are more open for those discussions.

You could see he had a sense of humor. I could detect that when he was a Yankees coach. I wouldn't call it a dry wit, but he had special ways of saying things. He'd give people nicknames, often for no apparent reason. He called me "Herbie." All I knew was that when he was with the Yankees, he called a catcher named Dennis Werth "Herbie."

In 1987, it was pretty obvious he might not complete spring training. It was painfully obvious he couldn't finish the year as

Dick Howser, pictured in 1980 when he was the Yankees' manager, sported a black armband in memory of Thurman Munson, who had died in a 1979 plane crash. Little did baseball imagine that Howser would be another of the sport's premature losses later in the decade.

manager. Just the fact that he was there, in uniform, said a lot about him. That was his nature.

Howser was competitive in golf or anything he did. He was interesting and fun to be around. He was a good person.

○ ○ ○ ○ ○

Matthews began as the Royals' number two broadcaster in 1969, chosen from more than three hundred applicants. He has been their number one announcer since 1976.

wowed by seeing college football's Heisman Trophy winner playing baseball. The NFL college draft in April 1987 saw the Los Angeles Raiders choose Jackson as a seventh-rounder. Only remote hope existed that the former Auburn star would switch sports, which explained why most teams ignored Jackson.

Ultimately, Jackson proved them all wrong. He joined the '87 Raiders, while continuing his baseball career.

In the 1980s National League, the Cardinals ruled the roost with three pennants and one world championship. Architect of those teams was manager Dorrel Norman Evert Herzog, known to St. Louis rooters only as "Whitey." The media loved his thoughtful, colorful approach to strategy, extending his nickname to "The White Rat." Despite an ever-changing cast of characters and a "bullpen by committee" that worked without a set stopper, he collected his third senior circuit pennant in 1987.

No Cardinal could corral MVP honors for 1987, though. Atlanta's Dale Murphy held on to the award for a second straight year. The gifted center fielder debuted in 1976, but failed in his initial position of catcher. He faced a mental block in throwing the ball back to the pitcher.

Murphy peaked offensively in 1987, swatting a career-high 44 homers. He trailed Schmidt in the homer derby by only 5, hitting 308 for the decade.

The Cubs received a free-agent gift in 1987, in the form of Andre Dawson. The outfielder presented the team with a blank contract when no one else would sign the creaky-kneed slugger. For the first time, a last-place team owned an MVP.

The Windy City saw history made on the evening of August 8, 1988. Permanent field lights were installed and used for the first time in Wrigley Field. The ballpark was the last holdout in baseball in accepting the idea of regular night games. The hopes of increased attendance and the fear that their home turf would be eliminated from postseason play (by being unable to host night games on television) motivated the team. Because of rain—which purists thought was nature's veto of the electrical addition—the game had to be completed on August 9.

However, 1988 belonged to the Los Angeles Dodgers and pitcher Orel Hershiser. "Clark Kent at least had a good body," the humble hurler once said when he was called a Superman. "I'm Jimmy Olsen." Actually, Hershiser became "Bulldog," an assigned identity. Then–Dodgers pitching coach Ron Perranoski explained, "We nicknamed him Bulldog for the very aggressive face… he doesn't have."

Hershiser hurled history with 59 consecutive scoreless innings, breaking the record of Dodgers pitcher-turned-broadcaster Don Drysdale. Drysdale was on the field to congratulate Hershiser following the September 28 event. Although it was never counted with the official total, Hershiser added more zeroes with an 8-inning shutout against the Mets in Game One of the NL championship series.

As a footnote to the championship, Hershiser appeared again before a national TV audience the next night, on Johnny Carson's *The Tonight Show*. The pitcher confessed that he sang hymns to himself during games, on the mound or the bench. Like a veteran catcher, Carson got one final brilliant performance from "Bulldog" that season: without

TOP: *Vincent "Bo" Jackson, a former college football Heisman Trophy winner, provided the Royals with sideshow power in the 1980s.*

ABOVE: *Eternally damned by Red Sox rooters for his fatal 1986 World Series fielding flaw, Bill Buckner continued to be an unsung hitting hero of the 1980s. Fans forget that "Billy Bucks" helped the BoSox to postseason play with 18 homers and 102 RBI.*

LEFT: *Roger "Rocket Man" Clemens collected consecutive Cy Young Awards in 1986 and '87. His '86 highlights included a record-setting 20-strikeout performance against the Mariners.*

REMEMBERING "THE KID," PAST AND PRESENT

As Told by Leland Smith

The first I recall taking special notice of Ken Griffey, Jr., was after he won the All-Star MVP award in 1992. I was on the field taking pictures for the Mariners' Second Opening Night, a celebration over the team's change of ownership. Then-AL president Bobby Brown was there to award the MVP trophy.

Before the presentation, I saw Griffey in the dugout, his hat on backward. He was goofing with the batboys, tickling them, away from the other players. When Griffey's name was announced, he turned his cap around, and appeared on the field with a dignified walk. He went on stage beautifully. Back in the dugout, he handed the trophy to a ballboy, then turned his cap backward again. His grin went from being picture-perfect to being a kid again.

I covered his future wife as a high school athlete who grew up in Gig Harbor [Washington]. Missy, who is now called Melissa, graduated in 1987. The next summer, at a teen dance club in Seattle, she met him. She didn't know who he was. This was his rookie year. Griffey told her to call, and he'd get tickets for her and her friends. She telephoned him the next morning and woke him up.

After they were married, I landed a one-on-one interview with Griffey. I finished all my questions, but he wanted to talk. He wanted to ask me all about what I remembered about Melissa from high school, her sports, her friends—everything.

He's something special. He doesn't take his fame that seriously. I wasn't an awesome fan, but I've seen my seven-year-old mesmerized. Then, I've seen Griffey through his eyes. My son Nolan came home from a book sale at school, saying he had to have a Griffey poster. When a kid gets that look in his eye, a dad makes $3.50 happen. I understand. My favorite player at that age was Willie Mays. They are both number 24, and they're both center fielders.

In Nolan's eyes, Griffey is real. We've been to games, and he's seen an actual figure. But I never got to see Mays play in person. Still, I remember the tinglies when he'd do something in a game on TV. Your chest puffs up, and you say, "That's my guy. I saw him do that!"

Nolan understands. The memories aren't worthless. We have something in common.

If I have a grandson who never gets to see Griffey play, I'd tell him how much the guy enjoyed being around baseball and

Long before Seattle fans were treated to their first division title in 1995, they could count on excitement any time "Junior" batted. Griffey was considered more than a team catalyst—his presence and gate appeal helped keep the Mariners from abandoning Washington in the early 1990s.

playing the game. Griffey made the crowd take notice, with a talent so incredible and so fun to watch. "The Kid" was a kid, a little boy in a man's body. And everyone says there has to be a little boy in you to play the game.

○ ○ ○ ○ ○

Smith is a freelance sports and outdoors writer living in Gig Harbor, Washington.

any accompaniment, Hershiser sang the hymn, "The Doxology."

While Hershiser was applauded as Series MVP, a teammate became a postseason legend with one plate appearance. Outfielder Kirk Gibson wasn't expected to play in any Series game. Hamstring problems and a strained knee made Gibson an unlikely star—or participant—in the World Series. His status changed with 2 out in the bottom of the ninth. After remaining motionless through a full count, Gibson's first swing produced a 2-run, come-from-behind homer against relief ace Dennis Eckersley.

As Gibson hobbled around the bases, his face seemed mixed with grins and grimaces. As his arms and fists pumped at his sides, Gibson looked like a weary cross-country skier. Gibson pushed teammates away as he crossed home plate, afraid they'd try to hoist him onto their shoulders. The strain would be too much. Gibson sat out the rest of the Series. "In a year that has been so improbable, the impossible has happened!" summarized NBC announcer Vin Scully.

Disasters of the natural and unnatural varieties hit baseball in 1989. Cincinnati's Pete Rose was banned from baseball for life after an investigation concluded that he had bet on baseball. Commissioner Giamatti issued a moving statement explaining the decision to expel the hit king, a decision that would keep Rose from the Hall of Fame. "The matter of Mr. Rose is now closed. It will be debated and discussed," Giamatti concluded. "Let no one think that it did not hurt baseball. That hurt will pass, however, as the great glory of the game asserts itself and a resilient institution

goes forward. Let it also be clear that no individual is superior to the game."

The fifty-one-year-old baseball philosopher, subsequently vacationing on Martha's Vineyard, saw his handling of the Rose affair become his last official act. Giamatti died of a heart attack on September 1.

His successor was Francis T. (Fay) Vincent, who assisted Giamatti as baseball's first-ever deputy commissioner.

Baseball began to look for the future in its past. The only AL team to continue to wear the beltless, double-knit uniforms constantly in 1989 was the Brewers. The Braves had returned to their tomahawk logo, and the Astros dropped their rainbow Technicolor jerseys.

Although the Mariners abandoned their trident "M" symbol and double-knit pajama-style uniforms in 1987, they needed another two years to add a resident superstar: nineteen-year-old Ken Griffey, Jr., the youngest player in the majors. The teen idol had begun as a first-round draft pick in 1987, complete with a $150,000 signing bonus.

History may hint that Kirk Gibson became the 1988 NL Most Valuable Player simply on the strength of his game-winning World Series homer. However, prior to his single heroic plate appearance, Gibson had powered the Dodgers to the postseason with 25 homers and 76 RBI.

Even at class-A San Bernadino, Griffey had star power. "What time is it?" the P.A. announcer would bellow.

"It's Griffey time!" called the crowd, whenever you-know-who came to bat.

By the end of his first season in Seattle, a candy bar was named after "The Kid." More than 800,000 bars were sold.

The Angels inserted their first-round draft choice from 1988 in their 1989 starting rotation, marking only the fifteenth time a draftee went straight to the majors without a day in the minors. The pitcher being fast-tracked was Jim Abbott, who had been a star with the University of Michigan and the 1988 gold medal–winning Olympic team. His amateur stardom was even more amazing, considering that he was born without a right hand.

The National League found its share of stirring inspiration in another lefty, Dave Dravecky.

Dravecky debuted with the Padres in 1982. A year later, Dravecky pitched two scoreless innings for the NL all-stars. In 1984, he hurled 10⅔ shutout innings of relief in postseason for the league champions. On July 4, 1987, Dravecky was swapped to San Francisco in a seven-player deal.

In January, 1988, doctors concluded that a lump on Dravecky's pitching arm was "probably benign." He went on to win opening day against the Dodgers. However, shoulder surgery in June was followed by an October operation to remove the now-malignant tumor and surrounding deltoid muscle in the arm.

Instead of retiring, Dravecky got permission to begin training for a comeback. Beginning in July 1989, the Ohio native tested his arm in 3 minor league starts. Three complete-game wins resulted.

On August 10, Dravecky returned to Candlestick for a start that many thought would never materialize. He lasted 8 full innings, earning a 4–3 win against the Reds. His lengthy outing was more than symbolic: for each pitch thrown, fans pledged to donate to a fund for a bone-marrow transplant for a local boy with leukemia. More than $115,000 was raised.

Five days later, on August 15, Dravecky tried another start in Montreal. After 5 shutout innings, the sixth spelled the end of the lefty's career. Facing Tim Raines, Dravecky's arm broke during the first pitch. Later, Dravecky said that he was concerned that his arm was no longer attached to his body.

The ill-fated pitcher couldn't participate in the team's divisional win, although he threw out the ceremonial first pitch in the third game of the championship series against the Cubs. Fate struck once more when the Giants won the pennant in 5 games. Dravecky joined the celebratory dogpile, and his arm was rebroken in the melee. On November 13, less than a month after doctors announced that cancer had recurred in the arm, Dravecky retired.

The Giants would face more than a lost pitcher during the World Series.

Facing Oakland from across the bay, the Series had the same geographic appeal that the 1985 Cards-Royals affair did. However, as Game Three was set in San Francisco, Candlestick Park's geography left a lot to be desired.

On October 17, an earthquake knocked out power to the ballpark minutes before the game started. A total of sixty-seven earthquake-related deaths occurred in the area, but none at Candlestick. Ten days later, after the stadium was declared structurally sound, the last 2 games were played to provide Oakland's sweep.

On more solid ground in 1989, Johnny Bench and Yastrzemski were elected to the Hall of Fame. "Yaz" was named on 94.6 percent of ballots cast. The Boston legend and the Hall were both celebrating their fiftieth birthdays. Yastrzemski's induction marked the first time for a former Little Leaguer to gain Cooperstown immortality.

Fact and fantasy gave baseball fans hope at movie theaters. *Field of Dreams* was one of the biggest motion-picture hits of 1989. The film, based on a W.P. Kinsella novel, introduced an Iowa farmer who built a ballpark in his cornfield. The ghost of "Shoeless Joe" Jackson appeared, along with other players, for one more game.

Like Hollywood, the real-life major leagues were readying heavy doses of drama for the fast-approaching 1990s. The only question remaining was over the number of happy endings available.

Baseball lore was filled with human dramas during the
1980s. California pitcher Jim Abbott was a classic case,
succeeding on the mound without a right hand. While the
press marveled at Abbott's victory over a physical disability,
his successful leap from the college campus to the majors
without a day of minor league seasoning was overlooked.

THE END OF A CENTURY

It took only one year to prove that the nineties would be anything but business as usual for baseball.

The Detroit Tigers introduced an import to their lineup. Cecil Fielder, a former Blue Jays prospect, had played in Japan in 1989. Conventional wisdom made Fielder's two-year contract for $1.75 million seem like pure folly. Far from baseball's buffed-and-hunky ideal, at an estimated 250 pounds, Fielder was considered overweight and overestimated. After all, he batted only .230 in 74 games during his last year of spotty duty with Toronto, playing behind first-base star Fred McGriff.

However, Fielder silenced critics with league highs of 51 homers and 132 RBI. The last Tiger to top the circuit in both categories was Hank Greenberg in 1935.

Baseball was embracing the past, using history as a stepping-stone to the future.

Rescued from the Cincinnati bench, the Mariners added Ken Griffey, Sr., to their outfield in 1990. Father and son set history on September 14 with consecutive home runs. Seattle fans soon began calling the duo "Ken Griffey and Ken Griffey Senior." Junior compared their abilities, saying, "I've always dreamed about being in the Hall of Fame, but I think my dad is going to beat me there."

In Texas, Rangers pitcher Nolan Ryan produced another baseball achievement. The forty-three-year-old spun his sixth no-hitter on June 11, streaking his streak of no-hit wonders to three straight decades.

Reliever Bobby Thigpen was baseball's busiest record setter in 1990. The White Sox stopper collected 57 saves in 77 appearances, the most in major league history.

The Reds rampaged through the World Series, routing Oakland in 4 straight games. The Cincinnati bullpen of Randy Myers, Norm Charlton, and Rob Dibble earned the nickname "Nasty Boys."

OPPOSITE, TOP: *Speedster Rickey Henderson returned to the Oakland outfield through a second trade with the Yankees in mid-1989, meaning that he'd start a new decade in a familiar uniform.*

OPPOSITE, BOTTOM: *Baseball's first father-and-son outfield team transpired with the 1990 Mariners, as two generations of Griffeys hit back-to-back homers in the same game. Although the younger Griffey was but a sophomore in 1990, he was drawing comparisons to Willie Mays and other greats.*

ABOVE: *While no one could guess Detroit slugger Cecil Fielder's exact weight, few baseball soothsayers had predicted his rise to AL homer king after a brief hiatus playing ball in Japan.*

pitch in a World Series game?" A tenth-inning single by Joe Oliver won it for the Reds, enabling Browning (still in uniform) to witness the birth of his son thirty minutes after the game's end.

The race and rivalry for baseball in 1991 didn't involve mere pennants. Cities were politicking to earn the two NL expansion franchises slated for 1993. Tampa Bay built the Suncoast Dome expressly for baseball. By April, more than twenty-two thousand fans had bought season tickets for a team playing only on paper. Also-rans in the metropolitan beauty contests included Buffalo, Washington, and Orlando. The winning sites, Denver and Miami, paid $95 million each for franchise rights.

Historic happenings dueled for the spotlight on May 1. Rickey Henderson swiped his 939th career base, breaking Lou Brock's record. Brock had been attending A's games, hoping to be on hand when the record fell.

But bigger headlines went to the forty-four-year-old pitcher who no-hit the Toronto Blue Jays for his unprecedented seventh gem. Nolan Ryan fanned Roberto Alomar for the final out. On May 15, 1973, Alomar's father, Sandy, had been Ryan's second baseman during his first no-no.

Television's two cable superstations combined talents to make baseball broadcast history in 1991. A May 13 game between the Braves and the Cubs saw Harry Caray mikeside, along with son Skip and grandson Chip.

Although Jose Rijo's two Series victories earned him an MVP Award, another pitcher upstaged him. Thinking he wouldn't be needed, Tom Browning left in the seventh inning of Game Two. His wife was set to give birth. After he had left for the hospital, manager Lou Piniella decided that Browning could relieve in extra innings, instead of starting Game Three.

"I was sweating," Browning said of hearing a television appeal by announcer Tim McCarver for the pitcher to return to Riverfront Stadium. "I was scared. What did I want to do, be at the birth or

LEFT: *Bobby Thigpen set an all-time saves record in 1990. Five years later, arm burnout would cause the reliever to try to revive his fortunes by pitching in Japan after being dismissed by numerous teams.*

BELOW: *Cincinnati would claim the first world championship of a new decade on the backs of its "Nasty Boys." The fiery bullpen of Rob Dibble, Norm Charlton, and Randy Myers (from left to right) gave manager Lou Pinella the mound strength needed to upset the favored Oakland A's in 4 straight games.*

Sadness loomed in San Francisco before the all-star break. Retired pitcher Dave Dravecky's battle with cancer turned more serious, as his left arm and shoulder were removed in a two-and-a-half-hour operation.

Baseball displayed its forgiving side in July, bringing former rebels into Cooperstown's fold. Grandstanding owner Bill Veeck was named by the veterans' committee, while the Baseball Writers' Association of America approved pitcher Ferguson Jenkins. Being charged in 1980 with possession of cocaine seemed like a permanent blot on Jenkins' record then, but the media was more forgiving of what now seemed like a common flaw amongst players.

Rene Arocha, a pitcher from the Cuban National Team, defected after a July exhibition against Team USA in Tennessee. Jose Canseco, from the same Havana suburb, paid for Arocha's plane ticket out of Miami.

Before the season ended, baseball's "statistical accuracy committee" met. The asterisk next to Roger Maris' home run record was officially removed.

Baltimore's Memorial Stadium was retired at the end of 1991, as was Tigers broadcaster Ernie Harwell. Neither was given a choice. Harwell had started as an O's broadcaster in 1954, for the first game played in the Memorial. The final game was won by Detroit, 7–1, but the old ballpark went out a winner. More than seventy-five former team members, from first baseman Boog Powell to manager Earl Weaver, took their positions on the field one last time.

Baltimore disproved the myth that baseball fans have no sense of history in 1992.

The new ballpark was built on hallowed ground: Camden Yards. Babe Ruth's father had run a tavern on the site. Archaeologists studying the location announced that a dig had produced what might be remnants of the Ruth family outhouse.

Inside the park (actually named "Oriole Park at Camden Yards"), the nostalgic outfield billboards, steel girders, and other timeless touches gave the new stadium hints of classic fields like Shibe Park and Ebbets Field. Even while empty, Camden Yards became a tourist attraction. Stadium architects working in Texas, Cleveland, and Denver dubbed the Baltimore palace a prototype for all future ballparks.

San Francisco's baseball tradition nearly became ancient history in 1992. Bill White, all-star first baseman of the sixties and longtime Yankees announcer, became baseball's first African-American administrator in 1988. Four years later, he was making the most crucial decision of his executive career. In August, owner Bob Lurie had sold the club to a contingent of Florida investors, ready to make the team the St. Petersburg Giants. White rallied other owners to block the sale until a local buyer was found.

Although grocery store baron Peter Magowan took over the team and kept it in San Francisco, manager Roger Craig retired before the new regime began. Craig had managed the Giants since 1985, inaugurating the cheer "Humm-Baby." Most importantly, he taught the split-fingered fastball to a legion of pitchers.

One of the first acts of the new ownership was to recruit free-agent power factory Barry Bonds. Bonds inked a six-year deal for $43.75 million, averaging out to $7,291,667 yearly.

Many of the Angels could have taken their team name literally in 1992, after a bus accident on the New Jersey Turnpike. Although no fatalities occurred among the dozen injuries, manager Buck Rodgers suffered a fractured elbow and knee, effectively ending his season.

On September 7, 1992, owners forced commissioner Fay Vincent out of office. White Sox owner Jerry Reinsdorf and Milwaukee landlord

Bud Selig led the ouster. "The players don't need a commissioner to protect them," Reinsdorf told the press. Selig, head of the labor relations committee, became a substitute czar. Finally, after seven decades of outside rule, the owners verged on eliminating the commissioner's position. Vincent's star fell when he convinced owners to end their 1990 players lockout and drop demands for a salary cap.

George Brett made 1993 his career finale. Supposedly, Kansas City dangled a $2.7 million contract to keep him playing in 1994, but he chose to become a team vice president. "I didn't want to go out and embarrass myself. And I wanted to go out on my own terms," he concluded.

Not since 1977, when the Mariners and Blue Jays were born, had baseball seen new teams. Now, the National League evened the balance of clubs at fourteen apiece by adding franchises in Denver and Miami. To broaden the appeal of both locales, city names were abandoned. Hoping to give the impression that one site wasn't favored over another, the "Florida" Marlins and "Colorado" Rockies were christened.

No one doubted that the Rockies would be popular. When the December expansion draft was held (with Atlanta pitcher David Nied being the first pick), twenty thousand Denver fans showed up to hear the Rockies announce their choices.

Spring training became a nightmare for the 1993 Indians. Reliever Tim Crews and stopper Steve Olin were killed in a March off-day boating accident that seriously injured starter Bob Ojeda.

The Tigers had been sold from one pizza chain millionaire to another. New owner Mike Ilitch reinstalled announcer Ernie Harwell with a one-year contract after his forced retirement in

ABOVE: *Bud Selig (left) went from Brewers owner to acting baseball commissioner after ousting Faye Vincent (right) from the post in late 1992. Owners had vowed Vincent's demise after he intervened in 1990 labor unrest. Selig held the dubious distinction of cancelling the 1994 World Series when labor disputes remained unsettled. Vincent circulated a biting autobiography among publishers after his forced resignation, then refused to publish the work after his angriest comments about owners were leaked to the press.*

LEFT: *Baseball's first black executive was the familiar face of Bill White. The new NL president starred throughout the 1960s as a solid hitting and fielding first sacker for the Giants and Cardinals. Later, his insight shined through when he became a Yankees broadcaster.*

1992. Harwell's second farewell campaign helped win public-relations points for a team owner who would plaster billboards throughout Tiger Stadium, including an advertising sign behind home plate that could change from inning to inning.

If anyone was a fairy-tale success in 1993, it was Mike Piazza. Piazza was a sixty-second-round draft choice in the 1988 draft, the 1,389th player chosen overall. His father, Vincent Piazza, was manager Tommy Lasorda's cousin, and Lasorda convinced the Dodgers to use their last pick on Mike. Uncle Tommy saw his relative win Rookie of the Year honors with 35 homers (a record for rookie catchers), 112 RBI, and a .312 average.

For the broken-record department, reliever Randy Myers gave the Cubs a taste of history, while living up to his "Macho Man" moniker. His 53 saves established a new standard in the National League.

Montreal's September call-up of outfielder Curtis Pride provided one of the 1993 season's greatest inspirations. "It would make me feel good to hear the fans," he wished out loud to a reporter once. "But in my heart, I know they are cheering for me." In 9 at bats spread over 10 games, the deaf slugger provided a single, a double, a triple, a homer, and 5 RBI.

The Dodgers strived to give baseball more international flavor in 1994. Despite never playing a day of minor league baseball, Chan Ho Park opened the season with Los Angeles. His premiere, on April 8, marked the entrance of the first Korean-born player to the majors.

All signs pointed to 1994 becoming a year of feats and firsts for baseball. The first-ever perfect game by an AL lefty was thrown on July 28 against the Angels. Texas moundsman Kenny Rogers was the record setter. Following the feat, he was introduced to the famed country singer with the same name. "I wanted him to finally know who I was," the pitcher said. "After all this time, I sure knew who he was."

At the midseason break, Tony Gwynn scored the winning run in the National League's 8–7 all-star comeback win. The Padres outfielder was an all-star back in 1987, the last time his league had won a Midseason Classic.

On September 14, acting commissioner Selig broke America's heart. Because of the impasse in labor negotiations, the World Series would be canceled. Since 1905, war, economic depression, or earthquakes hadn't been able to halt the tradition. Pulling the plug on 1994 meant that fans would have to wait for the new multitiered playoffs, complete with wild-card teams. Initially, the Cubs tried to get an injunction to stop the three-division realignment. At the time, AL division leaders were the Yankees, the White Sox, and the Rangers (leading with a 52–63 mark). In the National League, the Dodgers, the Reds, and the Expos owned first-place records.

Although San Diego remained out of contention since a 1984 pennant, master batsman Tony Gwynn continued to generate a one-man offense for the Padres. Gwynn's star barely glowed despite his stack of batting titles en route to an inevitable Hall of Fame membership.

When the 1994 season was shortened by the strike, Gwynn held an astounding .394 average after 110 games. Three hits would have upped his mark to .400.

In the American League, Seattle's Randy Johnson led the loop with 204 Ks for a third consecutive strikeout crown. The six-foot-ten-inch hurler, nicknamed "Big Unit," considered retiring after 1992, the year in which his father had died on Christmas day.

The media went stat crazy in the aborted season. Computer projections claimed that Frank Thomas could have been a Triple Crown winner. San Francisco's Matt Williams was in line for a run at the Maris single-season homer mark. At the season's start, Ken Griffey Jr., Frank Thomas, and Jeff Bagwell (the eventual NL MVP) all set paces to reach 60 homers.

Although few fans or sportswriters thought any meaningful stats would come of the affair, White Sox fans were set for the coming of basketball great Michael Jordan during the September call-ups of 1994. Jordan had spent more than a year at the double-A level, but announced his "retirement" because of the strike, and returned to the Chicago Bulls without a day in the majors.

Before the strike exploded, one of baseball's biggest stars walked away from the game.

Cubs second baseman Ryne Sandberg was Chicago's beloved "Ryno." A regular since 1982, when he broke in at third base, Sandberg was only thirty-four years old. Despite having $16 million left on a $28 million contract, he said goodbye. After seventeen years in organized ball, a superstar was admitting that he couldn't play simply for money. Sandberg had been hanging on through the 1990s, hoping for one postseason experience with the Cubs. When general manager Larry Himes fired successful manager Jim Lefevbre after 1993, Sandberg questioned the administration's commitment to win, and his fading chances for a World Series ring.

Outfielder Raul Mondesi was Los Angeles' third straight Rookie of the Year winner. Since 1979, seven Dodgers have claimed the award.

Settlement or not, a few teams started making big plans for the season that might not be. The Padres and the Astros engineered a twelve-player transaction. San Diego general

Everyone hoped the World Series could outdo the drama of 1993. For the second straight year, the Blue Jays were winners. Joe Carter's sixth-game homer off Philadelphia reliever Mitch "Wild Thing" Williams was memorable, and not simply because it won the title for Toronto. Carter galloped around the bases, gold chain flapping and fists pumping, followed by a flying leap onto home plate. "They haven't made that word up yet to describe this feeling," Carter said afterward.

LEFT: *Ron Gant was let go by Atlanta after the 1993 season when a dirt-bike accident and injury gave the team a contractual loophole. After a year's recuperation, free agent Gant became a vital power source for the 1995 Reds' division title. However, Gant was a mere bystander as the Braves won their first world championship—without him.*

BELOW: *With a spiral motion harking back to Luis Tiant, Hideo Nomo became baseball's biggest surprise in 1995. Not since 1965 had a Japanese citizen played regularly in the majors. Nomo added to the Dodgers string of Rookies of the Year, although early debate bubbled over whether a veteran from another league could be considered a "rookie."*

manager Randy Smith found a willing trader in Houston. General manager Bob Watson's boss was president Tal Smith, Randy's father.

Players returned without a new basic agreement, offering to start the 1995 season nearly a month late.

Following their unveiling of pitching hopeful Chan Ho Park and a parade of new talent, the 1995 Dodgers unleashed Hideo Nomo. At age twenty-six, the Japanese hurler didn't fit the stereotype of a youthful newcomer. Instead, he was a five-year veteran of the Japanese Pacific League, before he agreed to a $2 million bonus to join the majors. Nomo paid immediate dividends for the majors. Besides attracting throngs of new Japanese fans at home or on the road, Nomo battled for the league strikeout crown early on.

Across town, an era began to end that May. The Walt Disney Company purchased a one-fourth share of the California Angels. Owner Gene Autry, awarded the expansion franchise in 1961, had initially only wanted his chain of radio stations to win a contract to broadcast games. Nearly two generations later, Autry's wife said that baseball growth and financial demands had bypassed the days of individual owners.

Outfielder Tony Tarasco was part of the package that Atlanta had sent to Montreal for Marquis Grissom. Tarasco was another Braves prospect struggling for playing time in 1994. With the Expos, Tarasco contended for the batting crown in early 1995. He also drew international attention for his ritual of writing "C.P." in the dirt before each atbat. Tarasco, a former Los Angeles gang member, has dedicated his career to Chris Pickett, a teenage friend killed in a 1992 police confrontation.

Another Braves castoff became a 1995 Reds mainstay. Outfielder Ron Gant was dismissed by Atlanta after a dirt-bike riding accident that resulted in a broken leg in February 1994. Cincinnati gambled by signing the power hitter, allowing him to rest for one year.

The 1995 season didn't begin on a harmonious note, though. Many fans who did come back

Ryne Sandberg, unhappy with the front-office leadership of the Cubs, opted for a sudden retirement in June 1994. "Ryno," a ten-time all-star, returned to second base for Chicago in 1996, happy with the change of administration for the team.

booed all players to voice their opinions on the strike. The Mets home opener featured a unique demonstration. Three young men in white T-shirts labeled "GREED" jumped onto the Shea Stadium field. They threw dollar bills at players, then acknowledged the cheering crowd by standing at second base with raised fists.

When attendance slumped early in 1995, teams tried assorted measures to win back fans. Teams like the White Sox decided to have the home team take batting practice after the gates opened. For years, the hosts would take batting practice in privacy. "We're not clowns in a circus," Frank Thomas had once grumbled to the press.

One unlikely hero to emerge in 1995 was Steve Palermo. The former AL umpire hadn't returned to the field after suffering a serious gunshot wound in 1991 while trying to aid a robbery victim at a Dallas restaurant. Serving as a consultant hired by Major League Baseball, he conducted a year-long study of why a 9-inning game takes so long. He recommended returning the pitcher's mound from 10 inches to 13 inches, forcing hitters to stay in the batter's box throughout their at bat, and reducing the two-minute break between half-innings (designed for added TV commercials).

The glue that held fan support in place was Baltimore's Cal Ripken, Jr. Regardless of Baltimore's record, the team drew larger crowds on the road than did other clubs. Everyone wanted to see the last surviving member of the 1983 Orioles world championship team chip away at Lou Gehrig's durability record, 1 game at a time.

Ironically, fans began putting Cal above the team's success. When he reached career lows of 14 homers and 72 RBI in 1992, the media began asking Cal to take a break. History-loving fans saw it differently.

Philadelphia's Mike Schmidt was the only electee to the Hall of Fame in 1995. Early in his career, the slugging third baseman was asked by a reporter what he would miss most after he retired. "Room service french fries," Schmidt replied.

However, four members came from an expanded veteran's committee. Richie Ashburn, the fifties Phillies outfielder, nineteenth-century pitcher Vic Willis, NL founder William Hulbert, and Negro Leaguer Leon "Dandy" Day were included.

Leon Day's election was the most poignant. In becoming only the seventeenth Cooperstown inductee who had played in the Negro Leagues, the seventy-eight-year-old Day died just six days after learning of the honor.

Nevertheless, the enduring reputations of a pioneering executive, a once-overlooked black star, and a long-gone pitcher proved baseball's staying power for the twenty-first and all subsequent centuries to come. As long as fans remember how baseball once was, they'll know how the game should remain.

PHOTOGRAPHY CREDITS

Front Jacket Photography:
Top left & middle inset: ©National Baseball Library; top right & bottom left: ©Bill Barley/Superstock; middle background and bottom right: ©UPI/Corbis-Bettmann

Back Jacket Photography:
Willie Mays: ©The Bettmann Archive; Roger Bresnahn: ©AP/Wide World Photos; remaining photography: ©UPI/Corbis-Bettmann

Interior Photography Credits:
Title and contents pages: ©Focus on Sports: pp. 3 top & bottom left, 7 middle & bottom left; Sportschrome: pp. 3 top right, 7 bottom right; all remaining photos: The Bettmann Archive/Corbis

©Allsport USA: pp. 150 bottom left, 154 bottom, 161 bottom, 162 bottom

©AP/Wide World Photos: pp. 17, 24 both, 27 bottom, 86 bottom, 87 inset, 107 bottom, 128, 130 both, 131 bottom, 132 bottom

©The Bettmann Archive: pp. 8, 9, 10–11, 12–13, 13 inset, 14, 15, 16, 18, 19, 21, 22, 23, 31, 32, 35, 36 top, 37 top right & bottom, 41 right, 42, 43 both, 44–45, 50, 51, 53 top, 56 top, 63 top, 65 top, 69 top, 81, 89, 93, 97, 99 top, 100 inset, 113, 129 top, 145, 159 top

©Focus on Sports: pp. 120 inset, 125, 129 bottom, 131 top, 132 top, 133, 134 inset, 136 top, 137 both, 138 all, 139, 140, 141 bottom, 142, 143, 144, 146, 147 left, 148 inset, 149 all, 150 top left & bottom right, 151 inset, 152 middle, 153 inset, 154 top, 155, 158 bottom, 160 bottom left, middle & right, 162 top right

©Reuters/Corbis-Bettmann: p. 162 top left

©Bob Rosato: pp. 135 inset, 141 top, 159, 163, 165, 167 both

©Sportschrome East/West: pp. 147 top right & bottom, 152 top & bottom, 157, 158 top, 160 top, 161 top, 164 both, 166; Bob Rosato: p. 114 inset

©Springer/Bettmann Film Archive: p. 56 bottom right

©UPI/Corbis-Bettmann: pp. 25, 26–27 top, 26 bottom, 28, 29, 30, 33, 34, 36 bottom, 37 top left, 38 top inset, 38–39, 40 top & bottom, 41 left, 44 inset, 46–47, 48, 49, 52 both, 53 bottom left & right, 54 both, 55 top & bottom, 56 bottom left, 57 both, 58-59, 60 both, 61, 62 both, 63 inset, 64, 65 bottom, 66 all, 67 both, 68 both, 69 bottom, 70 both, 71 both, 72 all, 73 both, 74, 75 both, 76–77, 78 both, 79, 80, 82, 83, 84–85 all, 86 top right & left, 87 background, 88 both, 90, 91 both, 92, 94, 95, 96, 98 both, 99 bottom, 100 background, 101 both, 102, 103, 104, 105, 106, 107 top, 108–109 background & inset, 110, 111, 112, 114 background, 115, 116, 117 background & inset, 118 both, 119, 120 background, 121, 122, 123 both, 124 both, 126–127, 134–5 background, 136 bottom, 139 background, 148 background, 151 background, 153 background

BIBLIOGRAPHY

Allen, Maury. *Roger Maris: A Man for All Seasons.* New York: Donald I. Fine Inc., 1986.

Buege, Bob. *The Milwaukee Braves: A Baseball Eulogy.* Milwaukee: Douglas American Sports Publications, 1988.

Butler, Hal. *The Harmon Killebrew Story.* New York: Julian Messner, 1966.

Caray, Harry, with Bob Verdi. *Holy Cow!.* New York: Villard Books, 1989.

Cochrane, Mickey. *Baseball: The Fan's Game.* Mahwah, N.J.: Funk & Wagnalls, 1939.

Craft, David, and Tom Owens. *Redbirds Revisited: Great Memories and Stories from St. Louis Cardinals.* Chicago: Bonus Books, Inc., 1990.

Devaney, John. *Gil Hodges: Baseball Miracle Man.* Los Angeles: G.P. Putnam's Sons, 1973.

Dravecky, Dave, and Tim Stafford. *Comeback.* Grand Rapids: Zondervan Publishing House, 1990.

Durocher, Leo, with Ed Linn. *Nice Guys Finish Last.* New York: Simon & Schuster, 1975.

Flood, Curt, with Richard Carter. *The Way It Is.* New York: Trident Press, 1971.

Gerlach, Larry R. *The Men in Blue: Conversations with Umpires.* New York: Viking Press, 1980.

Gibson, Bob, and Lonnie Wheeler. *Stranger to the Game.* New York: Viking Press, 1994.

Halberstam, David. *October 1964.* New York: Villard Books, 1994.

Hirschberg, Al. *The Al Kaline Story.* New York: Julian Messner, 1964.

Kahn, Roger. *The Era: 1947–1957, When the Yankees, the Giants, and the Dodgers Ruled the World.* New York: Ticknor & Fields, 1993.

Luciano, Ron, and David Fisher. *The Umpire Strikes Back.* New York: Bantam Books, 1982.

Lyle, Sparky, and Peter Golenbock. *The Bronx Zoo.* New York: Crown Publishers, 1978.

Mays, Willie, with Lou Sahadi. *Say Hey: The Autobiography of Willie Mays.* New York: Simon & Schuster, 1988.

Neft, David S., and Richard M. Cohen. *The World Series.* New York: St. Martin's Press, 1990.

Nelson, Kevin, ed. *Baseball's Greatest Quotes.* New York: Simon & Schuster, 1982.

Okkonen, Marc. *Baseball Memories: 1900–1909.* New York: Sterling Books, 1994.

———. *Baseball Memories: 1930–1939.* New York: Sterling Books, 1994.

———. *Baseball Memories: 1950–1959.* New York: Sterling Books, 1994.

Peary, Danny, ed. *We Played the Game: 65 Players Remember Baseball's Greatest Era, 1947–64.* New York: Hyperion, 1994.

Porter, Darrell, with William Deerfield. *Snap Me Perfect! The Darrell Porter Story.* New York: Thomas Nelson Publishers, 1984.

Porter, David L., ed. *Biographical Dictionary of American Sports: Baseball.* Westport, Conn.: Greenwood Press, 1987.

Rickey, Branch, and Robert Riger. *The American Diamond.* New York: Simon & Schuster, 1965.

Seidel, Michael. *Ted Williams—A Baseball Life.* Chicago: Contemporary Books, 1991.

Shatzkin, Mike, ed. *The Ballplayers.* New York: Arbor House/William Morrow, 1990.

Slaugher, Enos, and Kevin Reid. *County Hardball: The Autobiography of Enos "Country" Slaughter.* Greensboro, N.C.: Tudor Publishers, 1991.

Smith, Curt. *Voices of the Game.* New York: Simon & Schuster, 1992.

Smith, Ozzie, with Rob Rains. *Wizard.* Chicago: Contemporary Books, 1988.

Snider, Duke, with Bill Gilbert. *The Duke of Flatbush.* New York: Zebra Books, 1988.

Tygiel, Jules. *Baseball's Great Experiment: Jackie Robinson and His Legacy.* New York: Oxford University Press, 1983.

Ward, Geoffrey C., and Ken Burns. *Baseball: An Illustrated History.* New York: Alfred A. Knopf, 1994.

Will, George F. *Men At Work: The Craft of Baseball.* New York: Macmillan Publishing, 1990.

Yastrzemski, Carl, and Gerald Eskenazi. *Yaz: Baseball, The Wall, and Me.* New York: Doubleday, 1990.

INDEX